RODIN

Rodin

BY YVON TAILLANDIER

THE UFFICI PRESS · MILAN

Title page: EUGÈNE CARRIÈRE: PORTRAIT OF RODIN
Oil, 1898
(Gift of the sculptor Dervillez)

Translated from the French by:
ANNE ROSS

PRINTED IN ITALY

LANDSCAPE IN THE FOREST OF SOIGNES. Oil-painting, 1872-1876. Rodin Museum, Paris

THE SCANDAL IN THE ROTUNDA

The woman was naked, and her fingers were groping in the vain hope of covering her back. A man approached and, seeing her protruding bones, flat chest, lowered, raddled face and her body seated on an unidentifiable lump which looked like mud — was it really mud? — he gave up the idea of finding out and turned away with an expression of disgust. In another part of this infernal place, two enormous legs supported the trunk of a colossus. The giant was swooping down upon the crowd. " Master ", began a little girl in a worried voice, when a shout of " Executioner! " interrupted her.
" Master ", she resumed without apparently having noticed the interruption — " Master ". But the wave of mutterings and unpleasant remarks once more drowned her treble voice. Her interlocutor, a stocky man of sixty whose admirers compared his beard to that of Michelangelo's Moses, and whom some unknown voice had accused of being an executioner, bent down towards the child. "Master ", she repeated once more, this time making herself heard, and indicating the metal giant plunging down on the crowd without crushing anyone because, like Zeno's arrow which flew without flying, he was

THE WALKING MAN Bronze, 1877 Metropolitan Museum of Art, New York

walking without walking, " Why hasn't he got a head? ". It was the year 1900, in Paris, and the World Exhibition was at its height. On the corner of the Alma Bridge, in a round tent where he had assembled more than 200 marbles, plaster casts and bronzes, François Auguste René Rodin, who is regarded to-day as the father of modern sculpture and one of the most eminent artistic personalities of the western world, was holding the hand of his young interrogator. They were wandering together through the noisy throng of visitors and ordinary people who were no less lively, teeming and aggressive than the statues he had created. Without apparently attaching much importance to them, since he smiled continuously, he was observing the public's reactions. To judge by the exclamations, some of which reached his ears, there was no doubt at all that in spite of his vast fame which was already becoming world-wide, his figure of an old woman weighed down with years and his acephalous giant, who stood 7 ft. tall, and with a head would have measured more than 8 ft., were creating a scandal.

A MARTYR TO INCOMPLETION

This public indignation surprises us to-day. Why were these works considered depraving and scandalous? They were certainly novelties, and have been since used as models, have stimulated a spirit of enterprise and have instigated the creation of revolutionary works by other sculptors. Thinking about the decrepit old woman, I am reminded of Germaine Richier's corroded sculptures which were created forty years after the scandal in the rotunda. As for the headless giant, who without moving gave such a strong and perplexing impression of walking, and whom I cannot help relating to Giacometti's filiform walkers, first shown to the public forty years after him yet walking with the same gay, determined step, he acquired fervent and distinguished admirers as soon as he appeared, or very soon after — notably a celebrated poet who was Rodin's secretary, Rainer Maria Rilke, and a young man who was to become one of the most effective representatives of post-Rodin sculpture — Brancusi.
There are however not only admirers who talk, like Brancusi or write, like Rilke. There are also those who prove their admiration by their works. In fact more or less simultaneously walking figures began to proliferate throughout the world of sculpture, and this trend, inspired by a walker lacking head and arms — for his decapitation is accompanied by this double mutilation, which makes the acephalous man armless too — was not the work of insignificant people. The greatest of the Fauves, Henri Matisse, in his brief period as a sculptor, made a statue in 1903 called *The Serf*. Brancusi said that he admired in *L'Homme qui marche* (*The Walking Man*) — page 6 — the way in which a volume (the headless, armless trunk) has been placed in space, that is, projected by two legs set apart in a way calculated to give the outline of a capital Y upside down, whether one looks at him in profile, full-face or from the back, or of a fork with its prongs buried in the earth. Matisse's *Serf*, even though less mutilated than Rodin's walker, (he has a head and upper arms, though his forearms are missing), also stands with his legs apart, making the same upturned Y. There is also an cdd character dated 1913 by Boccioni, one of the founders of the futurist movement, who looks like a mass of wood-shavings blown by the wind into the form of a person without arms, but with a sort of head, walking in a way which produces the same upturned Y or the fork with down-turned prongs. The same figure is to be found in *Le Carroussel-Pierrot* (*The Merry-go-round Pierrot*) also sculpted in 1913, by Archipenko, one of the first sculptors to use geometrical elements exclusively in his statues.

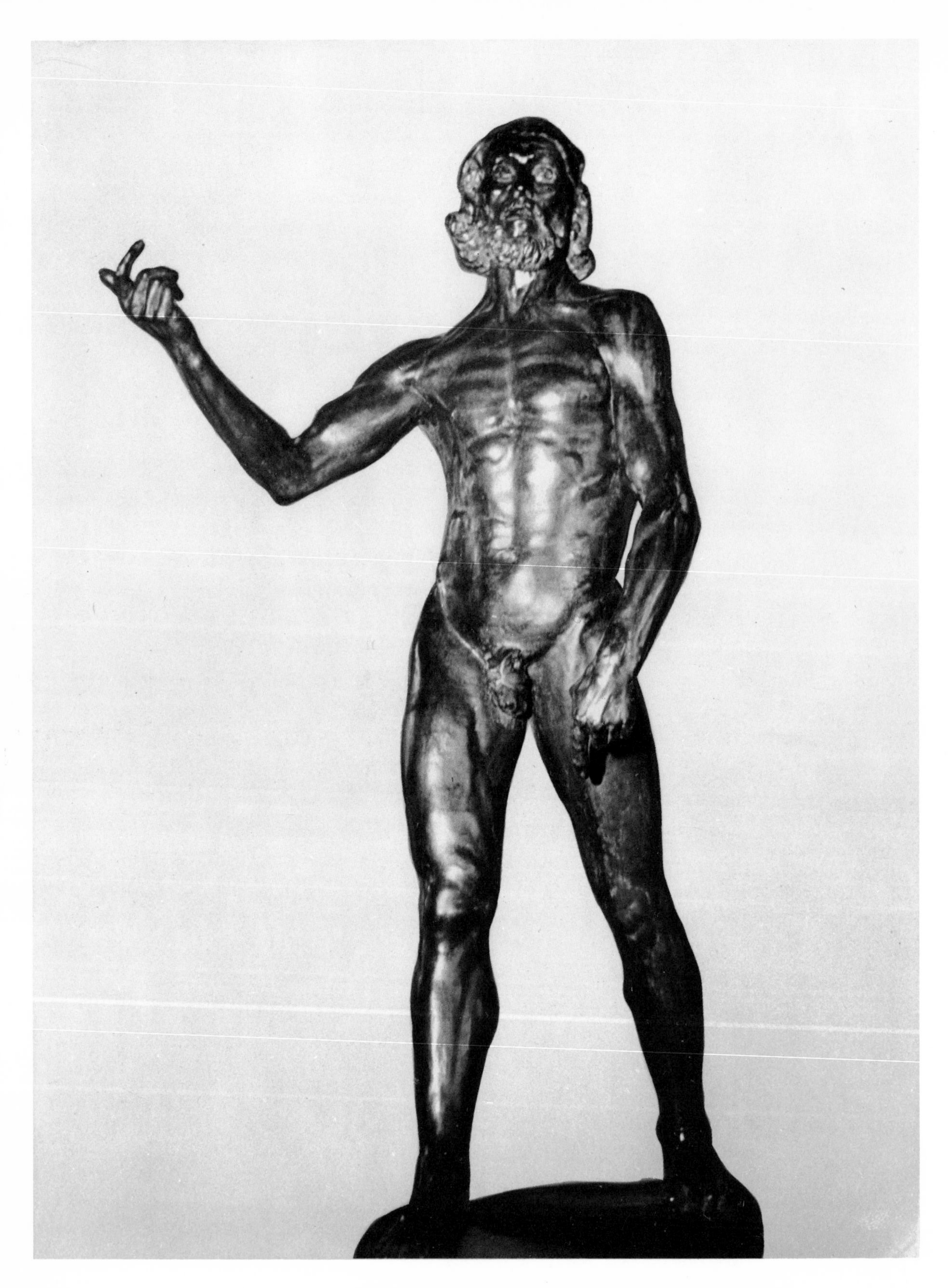

ST. JOHN THE BAPTIST PREACHING Bronze, 1877 Rodin Museum, Paris

Detail from page 8

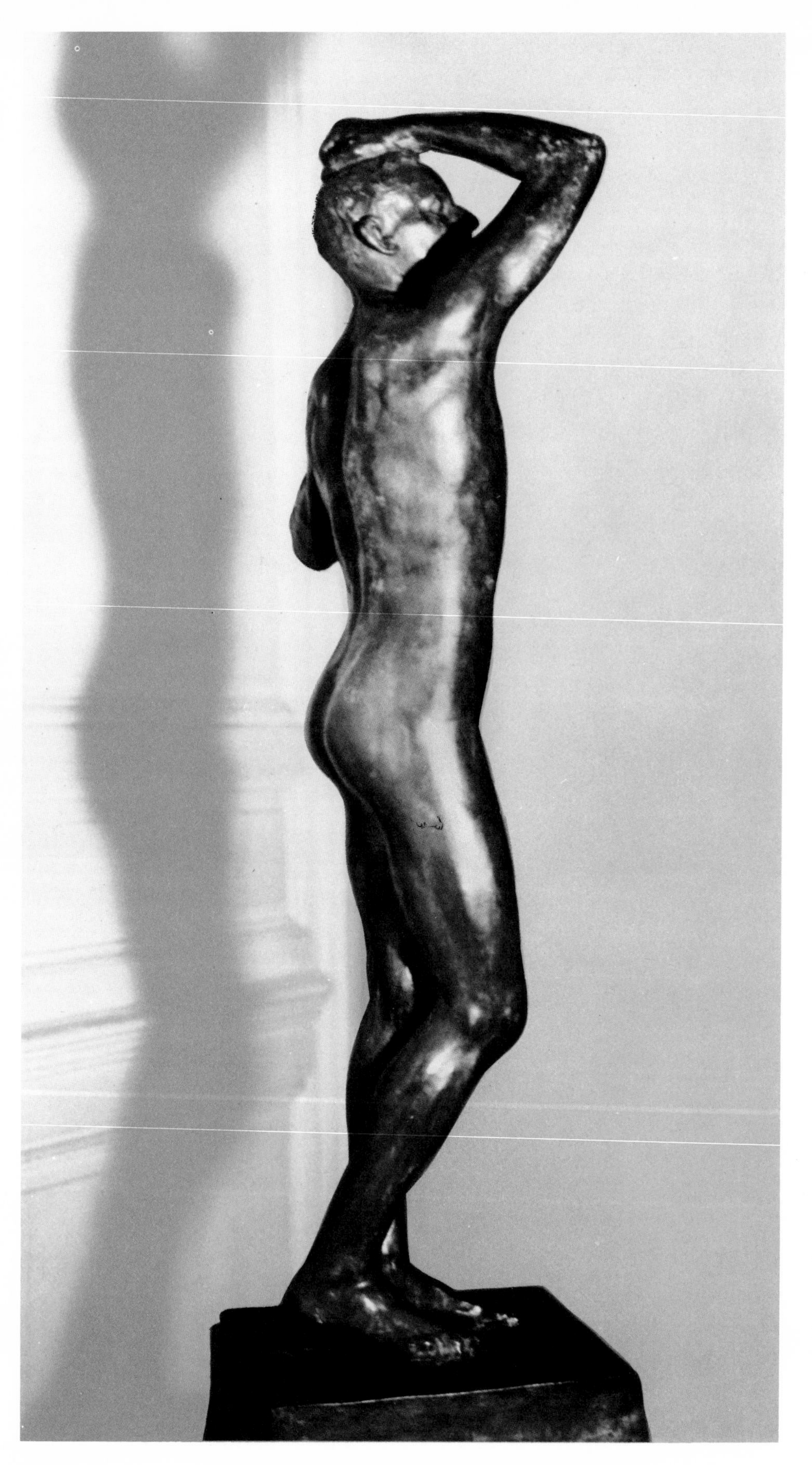

The Bronze Age
Bronze, 1876
Rodin Museum
Paris

If the little girl who in 1900 asked the sixty-year-old Rodin why his armless giant had no head, had not been too modest to notice that his sexual organs, at least in certain lights, seemed insignificant and even partially effaced, and to ask Rodin about this too, he would have replied that this did not make his giant any less potent. In fact he is still procreating, because I have recently seen in the studio of one of the best young sculptors of to-day, Jacques Delahaye, a walking figure with only thighs for legs, but which otherwise closely resembles Rodin's man. Besides, in a posthumous appraisal of the works of the father of modern sculpture, the headless, armless giant occupies an important position which is not solely attributable to his physical dimensions.

Sixty-two years after the scandal at the World Exhibition, a leaflet introducing an exhibition of seventy-two small sculptures and forty-two drawings by Rodin at the Art Institute of Minneapolis well summarizes the posthumous prestige of the great sculptor. " For twenty years, from 1930 to 1950 " writes the anonymous author, " Rodin began to be unfashionable among artists who in their purely formal experiments found the drama and passion which characterize his work embarrassing, but some years ago he was rediscovered ". The editor adds that this artist, whom he describes as a pinnacle in the history of western art, but who was so attacked during his lifetime, like Picasso is now receiving his just reward. This leaflet only contained one photograph, but to suggest to the reader by the reproduction of one work the whole sum of the creation of the greatest sculptor of the nineteenth century, the statue chosen is not *L'Age d'Airain* (*The Bronze Age*) nor *Saint Jean-Baptiste Prêchant* (*St. John the Baptist Preaching*), nor yet the prodigious *Balzac*, nor one of the *Bourgeois de Calais* (*Burghers of Calais*), impressive as they all are, but the walking man without a head.

A year later, Parisians saw two exhibitions devoted to Rodin's works, one at the Louvre and the other at a gallery specializing in sculpture, where the pieces shown had been strictly chosen because they could satisfy the demands of the amateur avant-garde. A few years before her death in 1959, Germaine Richier told me that in her opinion the greatest sculptor of all was Rodin " but ", she added, " that may make me sound a little old-fashioned ". The exhibition in the avant-garde gallery would seem a refutation of this criticism. Among the works selected was the headless giant.

If nowadays we hardly find his headlessness surprising, we are at fault. This work could be called, as Rodin called his monument to Balzac, the very pivot of his aesthetic, for the omission of the man's upper extremity played a decisive role in the evolution of sculpture which has led to its present state, but it also gave the headless creature a rich symbolism. This is why amid the tumult of the puzzled, angry visitors to the rotunda, the little girl was quite right to ask respectfully " Master, why hasn't he got a head? ". In his work entitled *Discovery of Modern Sculpture*, Jean Selz remarks that the mutilation of the *Walking Man* has given rise to the criticism that Rodin was incapable of finishing a work. This reproach would seem annoying to-day, because incompleteness is no longer considered a fault of principle. A contemporary of Rodin and of the impressionists, Edgar Degas, said ironically of the many pictures whose " finish " excited admiration " Certainly they have been finished, but can one really say that they were ever begun? ". This quip became famous, and one now considers that incompleteness in the aesthetic sphere is not a sign of insufficiency but rather a powerful means of arousing emotion or interest. In fact we are living in a world of beginnings. Our impression is not that humanity is achieving great things, but rather initiating them. On the other hand, we live in a world of invention, and a meditative person likes his inventive faculties stimulated in his encounters with art.

Detail from page 15

THE GATE OF HELL Bronze, 1880-1917 ▷
Rodin Museum, Paris

THREE SHADOWS Bronze, 1880
Rodin Museum, Paris

THE THINKER Bronze, 1880 ▷
Rodin Museum, Paris

This is precisely the effect of incompletion. When one contemplates the unfinished *Walking Man*, just because he has neither arms nor head one can imagine that this is no Rodin, but some ancient statue decapitated and shorn of its arms by the ravages of time. Besides, perhaps the example of so many mutilated Greek and Roman statues which Rodin admired so much — for instance the armless *Venus de Milo* and the headless *Victory of Samothrace* — seemed to him sufficient authorization for the mutilation of his bronze walker. Rodin had said: " Antiquity is supreme beauty ".

In the rotunda at the exhibition of 1900, observant visitors might have noticed a strange couple embracing (page 20). Were they a man and a woman, or two women? They are in fact a man and a woman, but the man is in the course of changing his sex. And what if the *Victory of Samothrace*, which seems to sail at the prow of a ship as the *Walking Man* seems to walk at the prow of some unidentified vessel, were herself to change sex? She might perhaps lose part of her wings and the dampened garment which clings to her body, but would indubitably retain the pinions which closely resemble the embryo arms on the torso of the bronze giant.

However incompletion does not only send one back in time; it also draws one into a conspiracy with the future. One does not only ask " What were his arms like? What sort of face did he have? In what disaster or what struggle did he lose them? ". One also wonders whether " this creature has not any arms yet. Perhaps I should make them grow, but how, and what should they be like? As for his head, if I had to mould it, what features would I give him? ". In short, one's mind, stimulated by incompletion, sees it either as the attribute of a ruin or of a building under construction, which one looks at in terms of the past or the future, and feels drawn to participate in the act of creation. This is very fashionable to-day. " Transformable " works are being created, works which one can change by altering the position of certain movable parts, so that one tastes an element of creative excitement. Rodin himself wanted everyone in the world to be an artist, or at least to have access to the artistic world, if only through craftsmanship, the extinction of which he was already deploring.

Such considerations were certainly unknown to his detractors, who levelled at him the same reproach as they were levelling simultaneously at Cézanne, and with which their parents and grandparents had tried to crush Corot who, answering those who demanded to know why his works were not finished, said (this riposte is also attributed to Vernet de Lyon) " And what do you do with infinity? ".

So the headless giant gives Rodin a place occupied by no previous sculptor except Michelangelo — that of a martyr to voluntary incompletion and, more widely, to that which is taken for formlessness. But since research into formlessness is a way to find form on a different level, this incompletion, or formlessness, of Rodin's was to give birth to countless new forms, and particularly to abstract, non-representational or obliquely representational form. In any case, the critics of his headless man, who is a true advocate of fertile incompletion, did not foresee that by carrying to its logical conclusion the principle behind the omission of head and arms and eliminating first the legs, then the division between chest and stomach, and finally the various distinguishing points which lead one to identify a human body, one would arrive at Brancusi's ovoid, at Arp's " nuages lisses " (" sleek clouds ") and at Stahly's pillars of hypertrophied glands. If they had foressen this, their horror would have made them doubly aggressive.

If one is no masochist, to be the victim of aggression can hardly be a cause for satisfaction. Rodin's feelings may perhaps explain his clear, though unemphatic reaction. That little girl who questioned

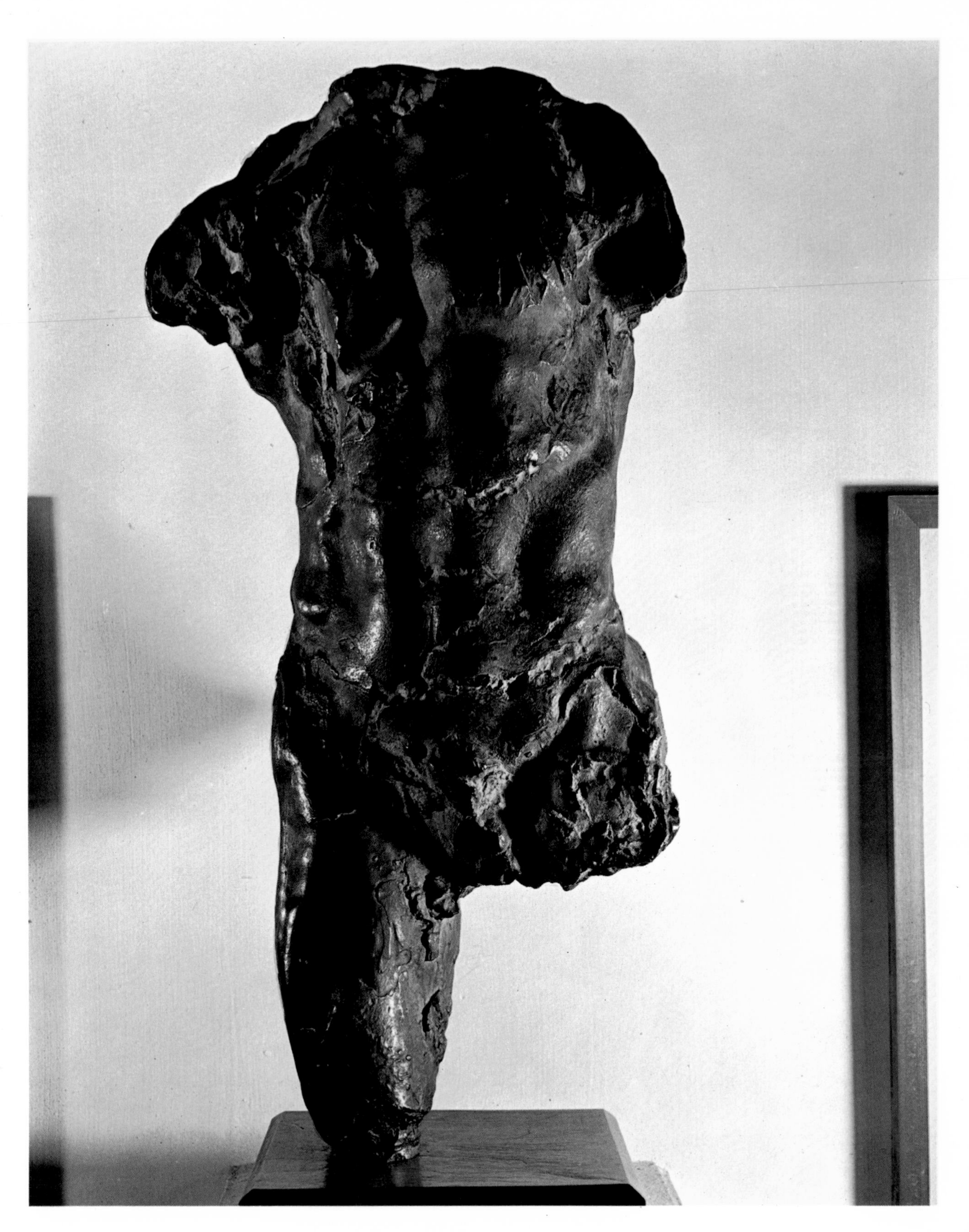

Male Torso Bronze Petit Palais, Paris

18 THE ABDUCTION — "I AM BEAUTIFUL" Bronze, 1882
Rodin Museum, Philadelphia, U.S.A.

MEDITATION Bronze, 1885 Rodin Museum, Paris

THE METAMORPHOSES OF OVID Bronze, before 1886
Rodin Museum, Paris

Women
Pencil and Water-colour
Bourdelle Museum
Paris

Despair Marble
City Art Museum, St. Louis, U.S.A.

DANAID Marble, 1885
Rodin Museum, Paris

STUDY OF A NUDE Water-colour Rodin Museum, Paris

him in the rotunda still remembers very well, more than sixty years later, the nervous and uncomfortable pressure of his fingers.
In fact, of what was he accused? The incompletion — taken as unintentional — of his *Walking Man* and the ugliness of his old woman?

OBSESSION WITH TIME

" Master ", said the little girl, " why hasn't your giant got a head? ". Rodin might have replied: " Perhaps because time has removed it ". And if she asked " Why is your old woman so ugly? ", he might have replied " Because she was also a giant — a giant of beauty, to whom François Villon wrote poetry. She was called 'The beautiful Heaulmière', but time has passed and, damaging her nearly as much as by beheading her, has left her in the state you see ".
Rodin took pleasure in describing Time as an executioner, even as he was accused of being one. This is one of the reasons why some strange things happened in that rotunda, so that the little questioner could have asked many other questions than the one about the headless giant. For instance she could have asked " What's that naked man doing on all fours? ". Rodin would have replied " That's a man eating his children. He is an ogre, a character from Dante's *Inferno* called Ugolin, and the group consisting of him and his victims is an enlargement of a detail from *La Porte d'Enfer* (*The Gate of Hell*) ". One can regard this ogre as a revival of the myth of Chronos or Saturn, the personification of Time, who also ate his own children. In any case Rodin might equally have replied: " That's a self-portrait ", because he seemed to devour or destroy his own works, like a modern Ugolin or Chronos. If the little girl, instead of looking straight up at the top of the giant had, like a mountaineer who starts climbing from the bottom to reach the summit, looked first at his right foot, she might have seen a protruding piece of iron, which had been used to strengthen the structure when it was nothing but a mass of clay. This apparent carelessness was a stylistic effect which has since been revived, notably by Robert Couturier, in certain works which include their entire framework. Rodin however just hinted, in his giant, at the possibility of a similar treatment, and doubtless the little girl, who could not know what the consequences were to be half a century later, would have dismissed it as unimportant. She would however have noticed that the rest of his feet and his calves, knees and thighs were modelled with the greatest care. Their surface is smooth and pleasant to the touch like a healthy skin. The swellings and indentations which mark the muscles and bones make a system of hills and valleys without sudden landslides or crevasses. From the top of his thighs, however, it all changes. Rodin, who respected anatomy (" Let anyone come and tell me if I have made an anatomical mistake! ") and admired the human body, loving its harmonies and carefully observing its smallest variations, metamorphosized himself into Chronos-Ugolin, giving the frightening impression of having grown fangs or talons. As though driven by a strange hunger he looked on his own child, his creation, as something to destroy. The genitals were crushed and on the stomach and the diaphragm two long, deep gashes which looked like fractures scored the body. On the back one notes divergencies from the usual contours of human physiology: the cleft dividing the buttocks is filled, while the buttocks themselves are by contrast caved in as though by a blow. On the flanks are strange pieces which might be bits of torn flesh and which as they hang seem to reweld themselves into the body. From

THE WALKING MAN Bronze, 1886 Bourdelle Museum, Paris

the front one sees a kind of crater, partly filled in, at the level of the groin, bruises at the top of the left thigh, holes in the upper dorsal region and a large cavity shaped like a comma at the top of the right lung. At the base of the left lung there is a twisted place as though the flesh had been pinched and the mark had remained. There is also a great vertical cleft starting at the base of the chest and going up, like a sword or dagger wound from the vertebral area. Under the shoulder, seen from the side, there is a kind of fork which traces three deep lines, and finally both arms have been torn out like plants pulled out of the ground — that is, appalling, palpitating whorls of flesh remain. Also where the head has been removed there is a gaping wound, which extends far beyond the surface of the neck to spread over the top of the torso in a great area of apparently putrid flesh. But to enumerate these actual wounds is nothing compared with the fact that they have been inflicted on a living person, and not on an unfeeling dead body, as in an anatomy lesson. This is a vital being, alive and upright, and the effect is that of the work of a torturer.

" Executioner ", said someone in the rotunda.

Apparently Damian, in an access of incomprehensible masochism, at the end of lengthy and terrible tortures, cried out " More, more! ". The *Walking Man*, having no longer a head, has no mouth with which to utter this fearful cry, but the very fact that he stands so terribly upright, like a cock which still runs about after being beheaded, seems to echo Damian's words on behalf of his lost lips.

This cry from a beheaded human body is not really an impossibility. The Spanish painter, Antonio Saura, has told me a story of his childhood in Madrid during the Spanish Civil War. He was looking out of the window at an approaching pedestrian when all of a sudden with a whistle a bursting shell removed the passer-by's head. During that seemingly interminable moment, which must have lasted a few seconds, he watched, his eyes dilated with horror, while the beheaded man continued to walk like Rodin's acephalous giant.

Jacques Bornibus, however, wrote in the introduction to the Rodin exhibition at the Gallery Claude Bernard in Paris in 1963 that " any purely dramatic interpretation (of the tortured, headless giant) is irrelevant ". So, there is no drama in the *Walking Man;* this seems an unacceptable paradox, yet it is true, though only from the viewpoint of detachment, which applies to a sculpture often placed at a distance from the spectator, as it applies to the impressionist paintings contemporary with Rodin. *The Walking Man* is dated 1877, and the first impressionist exhibition at Nadar's took place in 1874, just three years before.

I remember one day seeing two women looking at a Picasso painting. One was saying to the other: " From close to you see nothing, but from a distance it all falls into place ".

It is the same with Rodin, and more especially with the *Walking Man*. From a distance, it all falls into place, and Jacques Bornibus was perfectly right — " Any purely dramatic interpretation is irrelevant, because of the assurance of his posture and the obvious health of the body, which gives it vitality ". In fact from a few paces away this tortured body appears perfectly healthy.

In the Bourdelle Museum there is a little statue by Rodin, also called *The Walking Man* (page 26). This character has a head and two arms, and has suffered none of the injuries inflicted on his larger namesake, but he seems to go in fear of them. His head is bowed and his arms crossed on his chest make a diagonal guard over its rectilinear form and seem to be protecting it against threatened vio-

Fleeting Love Marble, 1886
Rodin Museum, Paris

lence. He is walking, but his movement seems a flight, and one doubts his ability to flee far when one observes the unusually unhealthy scrawniness of his left leg.

Yes, Bornibus was right: the large *Walking Man* glows with health compared with the small one, particularly when one sees him from a little distance and does not dwell on his injuries. What a splendid form he has, in fact, and what a magnificent interplay of masses, somewhat more complex than cylindrical shapes, but with a composition and swelling life which make him look even more vigorous. This is only true if one stands several paces back. When one comes closer, all one sees is sadism!

At the Hôtel Biron where the Rodin Museum is to be found, partly in the house and partly in the surrounding gardens and in a deconsecrated chapel, two walkers face each other at one end of the gardens, moving motionlessly towards each other. On the right of the entrance is *The Walking Man* and on the left *St. John the Baptist* (page 8). One can imagine that these are the same person at two different moments in his life, since St. John the Baptist was to have his head cut off and presented to Herod on a platter. The two phases or faces of this life are in fact combined in the same face — the radiant look of the Messenger of Christ and the downbeaten, corpselike air of the condemned and beheaded man. However to appreciate this one must undertake what I call in my *Voyage de l'Oeil* (*Visual Journey*) the educational promenade, that is, approach, withdraw and approach again, and never stand still.

From a few paces away what one sees is the relation of high and low, as St. John the Baptist seems to gesture towards the walking man, commenting "Look, his head has gone" and "Look, how alive his body still is". He thus seems not only to speak of the walking man but also of his own fate: "I began as a prophet; I shall be executed". This is also the dialogue or contrast between heaven and earth, spirit and flesh. We shall see how Rodin resolved this conflict in the years from 1898 to 1900.

For the moment let us walk about to gather knowledge. From afar (page 8) St. John the Baptist's head seems radiant, vital and forceful. From nearby (page 9) it seems conversely that life has already left it, and that its movements are no longer human. All Rodin's bronze portraits are similar, in that, like the face of St. John the Baptist and the body of the walking man, they portray torture if one examines them from close to, and without reflecting. They are all deepened, multiplied lines and accentuated features, recalling certain Byzantine portraits which look as though the skin has been stripped off them. To achieve the interplay of shafts of light on the facets, the flesh seems bruised, furrowed and torn. In short, here is sadism once again.

I remember that my youthful reaction to these portraits was to relish the tortures, and for a long time I felt guilty about my feeling of pleasure, until the moment when I realized that there is an irrepressible force in us which drives us to destrucion, but which one can conquer while seeming to submit to it, precisely through this type of delight which I felt in front of Rodin's multilated works, because it is better that a malevolent impulse should be satiated in this way and exhaust itself in imagination, rather than demanding of us real torture and blood. "This pleasure", I told myself, "is my way of attaining to sincere pacifism".

Certainly it may seem naïve to presume that if the public had understood Rodin better before the First World War and had loved his sadism instead of rejecting it hypocritically there would have been no war, but one cannot help thinking that the same men who shouted "Oh, how horrible!" in

Rearview of a Woman Water-colour Rodin Museum, Paris

Study
n Movement
Water-colour
Rodin
Museum
Paris

The Kiss Marble, 1886 Rodin Museum, Paris

The Kiss Marble, 1886 Rodin Museum, Paris

The Prodigal Son Bronze, 1888 Rodin Museum, Paris

The Eternal Idol Plaster, 1888 Rodin Museum, Paris

Bust of Falguière Bronze, 1897 Petit Palais, Paris

front of *Celle qui fut la belle Hëaulmière* (*She who was the Beautiful Heaulmière*), who cried "Executioner!" at Rodin when they saw his *Walking Man* and who thought the impressionists, Cézanne, Van Gogh, Gauguin, Seurat, the Fauves and the cubists hideous and frightful, soon after acquiesced in four years of world war, and that divorce between art and the public coincides exactly with the escalation of armed conflict.

Rodin's beneficent sadism is not always as obvious as it is in his bronzes, such as the bust of Falguière (page 36) or Legros (page 51) among others, or that portrait of Clémentel which I admired as a young man in the courtyard of the town hall at Riom. He does not always show himself so clearly as the reincarnation of the cruel Chronos — Time with his destroying scythe become sculptor. He sometimes speaks of Time more contemplatively or more sentimentally. The little girl so intrigued by the headless giant would also have been surprised by the acrobatics of a strange marble couple called *Fugit Amor* (*Fleeting Love*) — page 28. The theme of the couple occurs frequently in Rodin's work, allowing him not only to express his sensuality but also from the technical point of view to create massive sculptures, only slightly perforated, which would have satisfied Michelangelo's maxim: " A statue thrown from the top of a mountain should arrive at the bottom unbroken ". This massiveness also allowed Rodin (*would* Michelangelo have approved?) to stress the contrast between a very compact block and the arm or head which emerges from it. The couple who bears the title which evokes the transitory nature of love lie on an almost unworked block of stone reminiscent of a bed, a rock worn by the tide or the tide itself, on which the man, lying face down, strives to hold back a woman who is slipping away from him like a fish. She is no siren, but an anti-siren, who is no longer trying to seduce but to escape the bonds woven by her seduction. Time, which destroys love as it destroys life, has done its work.

Rodin also thought of Time in the sense of history, and is thus a forerunner of what is to-day called narrative art. Talking with one of his intimates, he explained at length that painting and sculpture could in the context of history vie with literature and music, saying that sculpture belonged to the dimension of time as well as to that of space. He takes as an example of this the six *Burghers of Calais*, commissioned in 1885 and erected in 1895 (pages 46 and 47). The expression on the faces and in the attitudes of these six men who to save their city agreed to be executed by the conquering enemy, can be considered in the narrative sense. In his movements and in his facial expression each burgher personifies one of the various stages of a deliberation which began in despair and ended in stoical resolution. Each statue is thus the equivalent of a chapter in a book or a paragraph in a lecture. The *Walking Man* can also be regarded in this way, for not only is it legitimate to ask: Where has he come from? where is he going? or even where is he? (since a naked man walking without head or arms could hardly be found in a normal place) but also to the little girl's question about his absence of head Rodin could have answered " Because he is telling a story of destruction which unfolds like a three-act tragedy: Act One, The Legs — all is calm and smooth. Act Two, The Trunk — the body is attacked, hacked, torn (the action accelerates). Act Three, Mutilations and Executions — the head and arms disappear. In dramatic terminology this is called the Catastrophe ".

There was nothing to prevent Rodin adding " You will see. I have made another sculpture of the same type in the form of a monument, commissioned by the Committee of the Society of Men of Letters on 6th July, 1891, on the initiative of Emile Zola, who was then President of that society. It

Woman Seated Pencil and Water-colour, c. 1900 Rodin Museum, Paris

Nude Seated
Pencil and
Water-colour
c. 1900
Rodin
Museum
Paris
▷

M.R
7145

PYGMALION AND GALATEA Marble, 1889 Metropolitan Museum of Art, New York

NIOBE
Marble
c. 1900
The Toledo
Museum
of Art
Toledo
U.S.A.

Two Women
Study
Pencil and
Water-colour
Metropolitan
Museum of Art
New York
◁

Two Women Study Pencil and Water-colour Bourdelle Museum, Paris

DESPAIR
Bronze, 1890
Rodin Museum
Paris
◁

▷
NUDE
REARVIEW
Pencil
Rodin Museum
Paris

The Burghers of Calais Bronze, 1884-1886
Rodin Museum, Paris

The Burghers of Calais Bronze, 1884-1886 ▷
Rodin Museum, Paris

took me eight years to finish. I exhibited it at the National Society, and the Committee of the Society of Men of Letters refused it in the following terms: ' The Society of Men of Letters with duty and regret protest against the rough draft which Monsieur Rodin is exhibiting at the Salon, in which it refuses to recognize a statue of Balzac '."

" THE GARDEN OF TORTURES "

Balzac drank coffee, slept little, worked much. When he died at the age of 51 he had an enormous stomach, which is the central theme of the first draft of Rodin's monument to him. This protuberant abdomen gave the sculptor the opportunity to create one of those magnificent swelling volumes which, according to one of the greatest cubist sculptors, Henri Laurens, looked like juicy fruits. The rest of the figure, with hypertrophied muscles, expresses strength and is in fact a tour de force, because Rodin has succeeded in making a resplendent figure out of a fifty-year-old who had never been a beauty.

At this point the monument could have been considered finished and the sculptor should have been content. But obviously he was not, for he continued working. He wanted to dress Balzac. First he thought of putting him in a frock coat, but rejected the idea, and was not sure what to do. The voice of one of his assistants, therefore the voice of a subordinate (like the serpent in Genesis, and like it, destined to become famous) suggested: " Master, why not drapery? ". Rodin was too much a realist to dress a nineteenth-century writer in Greek or Roman robes, so the voice spoke again. ' Why not a dressing-gown? " asked Bourdelle.

The die was cast, and Rodin covered Balzac in his dressing-gown, though others called it a homespun robe. Whatever the cloth, this vague, seemingly mineral shape (page 89) engulfed everything, arms, legs, stomach, leaving only the head free. This head, which is set on a strange geological phenomenon — a mountain, Miro called it — is another example of Rodin's sadism. This is the same theme as in the *Walking Man*, but in reverse. If the little girl, instead of looking at the headless giant, had been looking at the disembodied novelist, she would certainly have asked " Master, why hasn't he got a body? " and Rodin, ignoring the scholars' maxim that repetition is no explanation, could have answered her, in order to dispose of an importunate question, that *Balzac* and the *Walking Man* were not his only examples of execution and mutilation, or of showing wounds.

One of his first sculptures — one cannot help seeing an omen in this — is dated 1864 and is of a man with a broken nose. In 1885 he sculpted another man's head, not with a broken nose, but with the right ear missing.

The Walking Man can be thankful to have two legs, because there is another bronze character whom one can see to-day in the Petit Palais Museum in Paris (page 17) who looks like his brother in misfortune, since like his more famous relation he is missing his head and arms, and his chest and stomach bear the same wounds and ugly scars. If there is any joy in walking in this condition, he is ignorant of it, for his left leg is totally missing and of his right only the thigh remains, on which he stands like a flower on its stalk.

Even he should not complain, for if there is consolation to be found in the existence of a greater misfortune than one's own, it is his. There is a young girl, headless, who bears the marks of her hands

The Eternal Spring Bronze, 1884 Rodin Museum, Paris

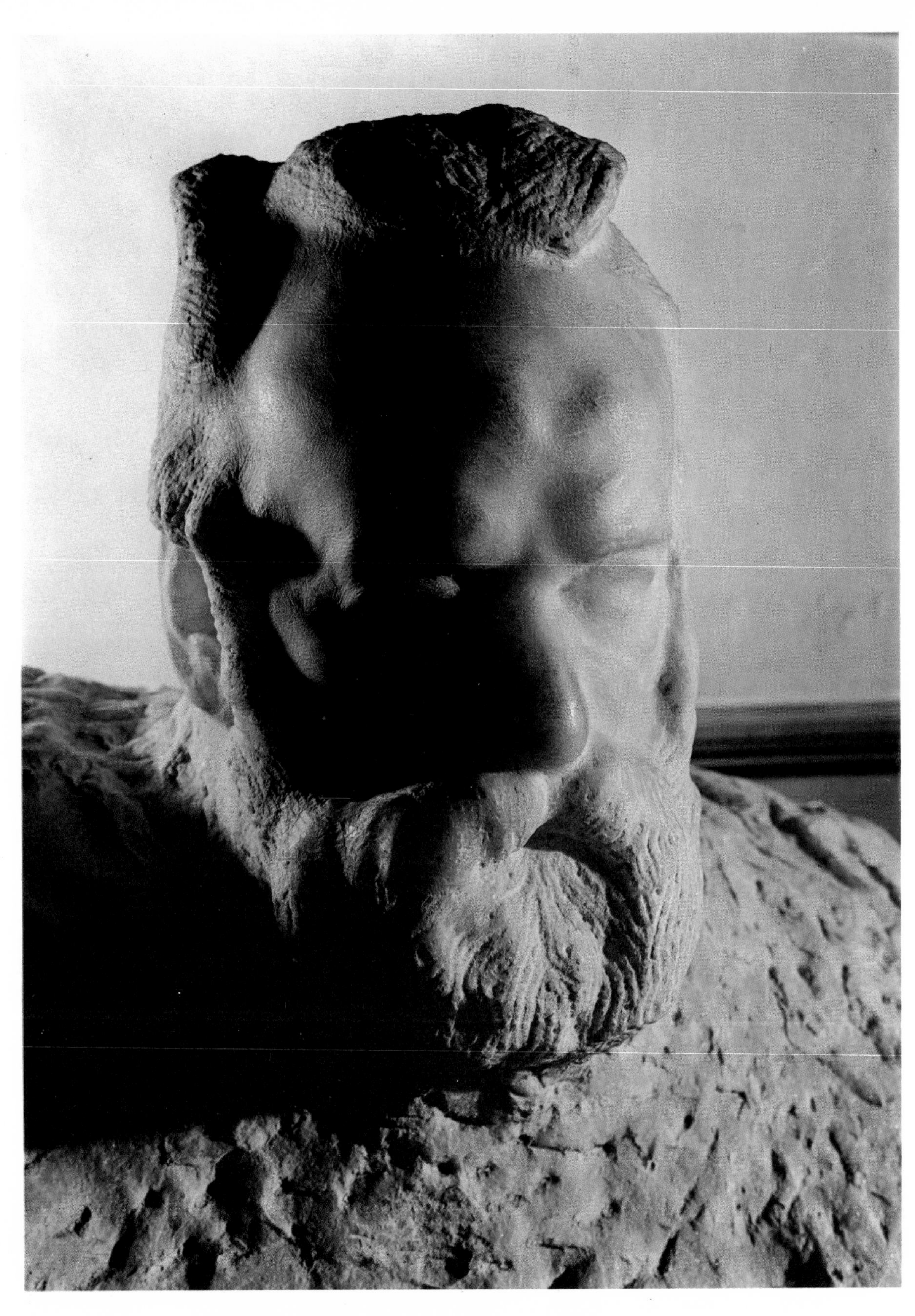

Victor Hugo Marble, 1883 Rodin Museum, Paris

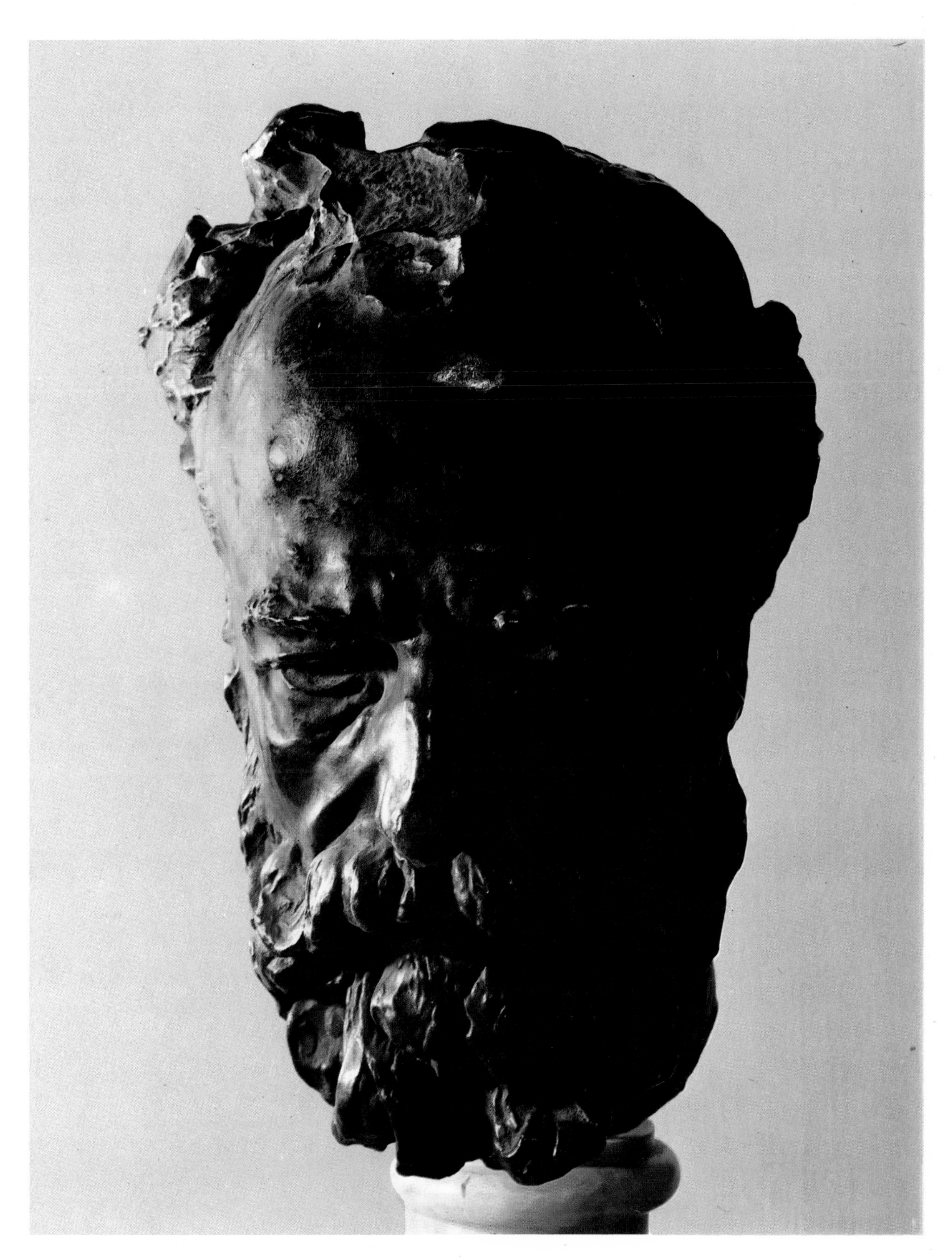

Alphonse Legros   Bronze, 1881   Rodin Museum, Paris

on her flanks, but lacks both arms and both legs. A headless young man of the same year — 1882 — is reduced to exactly the same condition.

An attentive observer of Rodin's work can note mutilated creatures in the stances of acrobats, like the headless woman called *Figure Volante* (*Flying Figure*) — 1891 — who holds her right thigh in her right hand, and has only her left forearm, stuck to her body, while her legs seem to be swimming or flying. Among many others, there are series of mutilated creatures. At the top of *La Porte d'Enfer* (*The Gate of Hell*) are are three characters, three men with bent heads known as *Les Trois Ombres* (*The Three Shadows*) — page 13. They resemble each other minutely, like triplets, but if one examines them closely one realizes that this similarity goes beyond that of triplets, and that they are, in fact, one and the same person, turning around himself, and that the group, sculpted in 1880, is in reality the analysis of one movement in its various stages, such as the futurists were to portray thirty years later. Until now no sadism can be discerned, but when one looks more closely one ascertains that when sculpting this group of three characters, or three views of one character in a more or less rectangular form, Rodin made each of them bend his head beyond the limit of physical possibility, so that one is led to think of three hanged men who have been resuscitated but who show their recent suffering in the abnormality of their necks.

Even from a distance they are impressive, not only on account of this anomaly but particularly because their three left arms converge, as do three arms belonging to fisherman apostles in Raphael's *Miraculous Draft of Fishes* as they draw the bursting net out of the water. Here the convergence of the arms was designed to fill a small space on the canvas which otherwise would not have been noticed, at least at first glance, and which in fact was the vertex of the miraculous draft as it emerged from the water. In Rodin's composition the convergence had the same significance. The three arms of the *Shadows* constitute an arrow which directs attention towards *The Thinker* and the *Hell* on which he looks down. To make this arrow sharper still Rodin, faithfully living up to his name of executioner, has cut off their three left hands. But this is not all, for the arrow itself needs to be stressed, and this Rodin does with a leg, belonging to one of the three, the knee of which is bent in such a way that it points to the three arms which point to *The Thinker* who points towards *Hell.* So that the point of this knee should look like an arrow and that it directional significance should be clear, Rodin not only put his personage in a difficult, contorted position which emphasized the indicating limb, but his right hand lightly veils the movement of the thigh. This method can be noticed in another sculpture called *Adam ou le Premier Homme* (*Adam or the First Man*) — page 62 — a reincarnation of the *Shadows*, different however in that the *First Man* is not pointing to anything, that his left arm falls vertically instead of being stretched out obliquely, and that his right hand exists. Rodin had ruthlessly cut off the Shadow's right hand, and as *The Shadows* are acknowledged as a single person, so the amputation of one hand at the wrist has led to the amputation of two others (page 14).

Thus *The Thinker* is in no danger of passing unnoticed, nor *Hell* of being forgotten.

THE DESTRUCTION OF CLASSICAL MAN

Who is *The Thinker* and what is this hell over most of which he broods, while a lesser part surrounds him without his seeming to be wholly its captive? The commonplace reply is that this is the hell of

THE HAND OF GOD Marble, 1898 Metropolitan Museum of Art, New York

THOUGHT
Marble
1898
Rodin
Museum
Paris

Mozart Marble, 1910 Rodin Museum, Paris

Bust of Mme. Vicuna Marble, 1884 Rodin Museum, Paris

Dante's *Divina Commedia*, but *The Thinker* is clearly contemplating the infernal regions. Is it likely that he knows Dante?

I was wondering along these lines one day in the gardens of the Rodin Museum. To my left, in the open air, was *The Gate of Hell* with *The Thinker* in his small-scale form. To my right, on a raised pedestal, the same *Thinker*, but larger than life. Looking at these two intellectuals, the large and the small, the thought occurred to me that Dante was a classic, and that to be acquainted with a classic one has to have attended a class. Regardless of his size, *The Thinker* seemed to me in spite of his name a wholly physical being, to whom the so-called cultural sphere must have been completely foreign (pages 12 and 15).

In 1876, four years before he sculpted that powerful body in which intellectual culture and meditation seem so misplaced, Rodin modelled the upright body of a young man, who seemed to have just awakened. With the help of its title, *L'Age d'Airain* (*The Bronze Age*) one usually interprets it as a symbol of man's awakening to consciousness, but though youth goes well with the idea of awaking, it goes less well with that of human brutishness touched for the first time with subtlety of spirit. This brutishness which is missing from *The Bronze Age* abounds in *The Thinker*. From some angles his outline is a zigzag line which recalls lightning and tempest, as though this seated man was prey to some internal storm, or the personification of the storm itself in which the first human ideas were to be born. In other words, he would be a representative of prehistoric man, the caveman. Caves occur as a frequent theme in Rodin's work, in the principle of composition governing the ' bracket ' form he likes to use — a concave form which gives a cavernous or corolla-like scoop to the human body, making Rodin a forerunner of Pevsner. Rodin's works often suggest prehistoric art. His drawings, though they herald Matisse, look as though they have been scratched on the uneven surface of rupestral caves. The divisions of line and colour, which make one think of Dufy, powerfully evoke the dissociation produced in an image by its movement, while movement is one of the characteristics of cave-drawings which most surprises the experts.

Is not *The Thinker* nude because he belongs to a society which had not yet invented clothes? But why did Rodin, in an age when clothing had long existed, persist in concentrating on that primitive era when man went about without any protective covering? Perhaps because he is a creator, and feels the vulnerability of his original ideas. Another sculpture (page 54) which at least in subject is the feminine counterpart of *The Thinker*, since she is entitled *La Pensée* (*Thought*), represents a female head just emerged from a rectangular prism of roughhewn marble. This one could describe as thought struggling with matter — the allegory of the first stirrings of creative ideas.

Creation has many other, equally challenging, aspects, so why was Rodin especially interested in this one? All his incomplete marble statues can express the same idea — that of beginnings or birth. To this question Rodin replied that " a whole new world is pulsing ". What is this world, still in prehistory? What is its connection with *The Thinker* and *The Gate of Hell*? " I know ", said Rodin, " that at this moment man is suffering ". Is this the suffering depicted in the panels of his infernal gate? Is it the suffering of Rodin's own times, which did not differ greatly from that of to-day? Is the hell which his Dantesque gate portrays not that of his century and ours? Does *The Thinker* not ponder on the events of his day and ours? The hungry figure of Ugolin devouring his children is not only a revival of the myth of Chronos in the Divine Comedy; it is a hideous image of a hideous and as

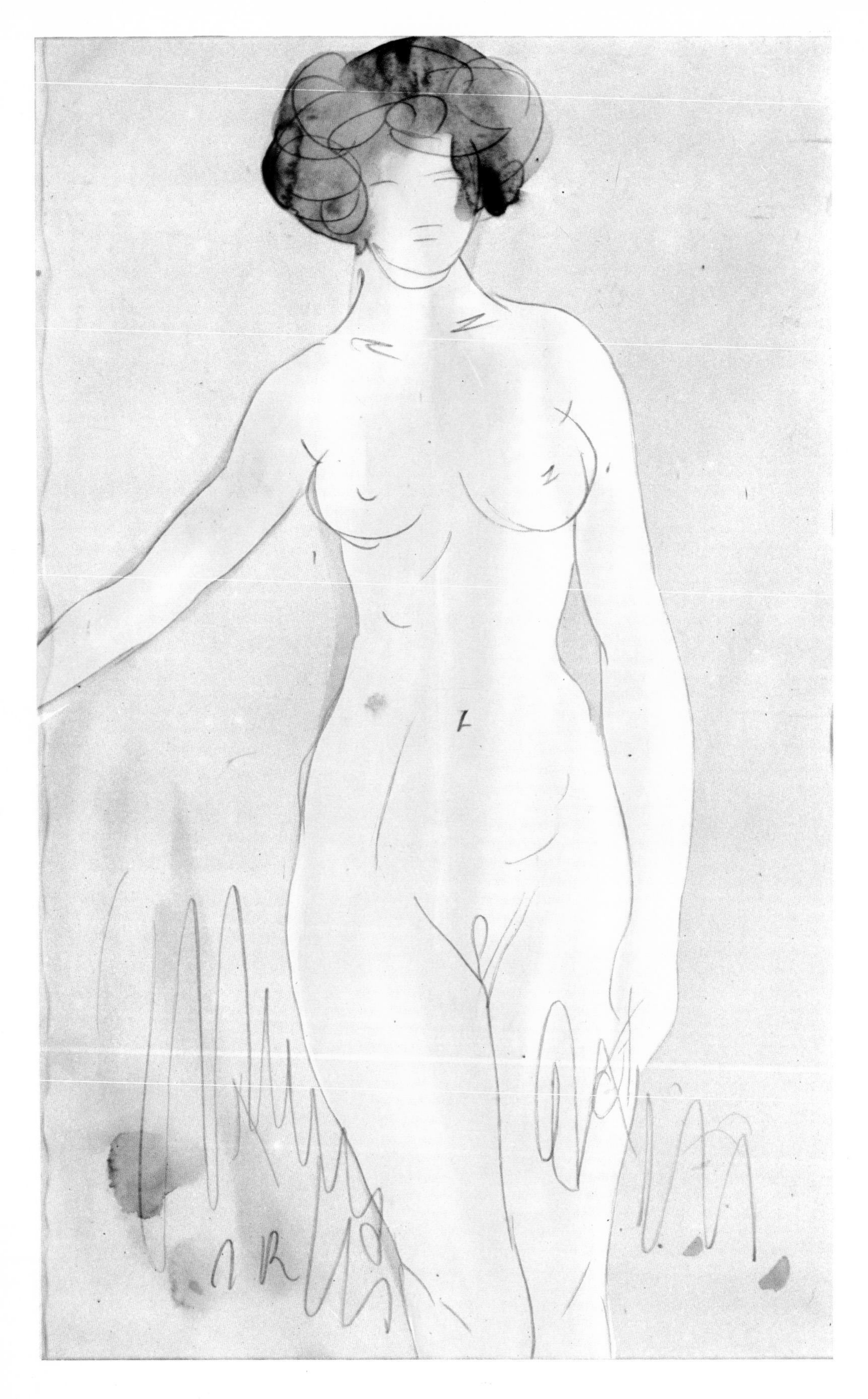

Red-Haired Woman Standing
Water-colour
Petit Palais
Paris

STUDY OF A NUDE Water-colour Rodin Museum, Paris

yet unresolved problem — that of world hunger. *The Martyr*, another character portrayed on the gate, is also still topical; we cannot boast that martyrs are extinct on our planet. *La Danaide* (page 23) belongs in classical mythology to a group of fifty sisters condemned to eternally refilling a barrel which emptied itself as soon as it was full. According to mythologists, she represented irrigation, which requires endless repetition of the same labour. Perhaps labour is the key-word. Before creating *The Gate*, observes Jean Selz, Rodin had conceived the idea of a monument, which at first glance had no connection with that which the State was later to commission from him and which caused him to abandon his first idea. But did he entirely abandon it? Can one not see traces of it in *The Gate of Hell*? *The Thinker*'s muscles make of him either an athlete or a manual labourer; perhaps some manoeuvre or just a daily task is afoot. If he has sat down to think, it is because he is accustomed to stand, and his job makes contemplation an unusual exercise for him. What is he thinking about? Might not the subject of his sombre thoughts be the poverty of the working classes in Rodin's day? The condemned of the soil, the convicts of hunger, as they are called in the words of a famous song, could they not be symbolized by the tortured throng which populates the panels of the dantesque door? Rodin was nine when Karl Marx wrote his *Eighteenth Brumaire of Napoléon Bonaparte*. He lived through attempted assassinations by anarchists and the development of the socialist movements. At the moment when he first became internationally famous the voice of Jean Jaurès was to be heard. Did he hear it? Great creative artists cannot stand entirely aside from the major movements which animate the society to which they belong. He died in the year of the Russian Bolshevist Revolution, and its triumph was also in a way his triumph, since the monument which he thought of raising was to be dedicated to the glory of labour. Thus *The Thinker* — who officially is also *The Poet* — would be in fact a manual labourer, a man of physical work, thinking how to escape from oppression and already beginning to succeed, thanks to an upheaval which revealed his morphological origins. He sits, like a whole series of Michelangelo's people who also belong in the realm of thought, such as the sculpted Moses on the tomb of Julius II and the Lorenzo II de Medici, also called The Thinker, or the paintings of the prophets Jeremiah and Isaiah in the frescoes of the Sistine Chapel. The Michelangelo character who most closely resembles Rodin's *Thinker* is however to be found in the famous *Last Judgment* painted on the end wall of the Sistine Chapel, which is nearer to Rodin's *Gate of Hell* than any other work of the past. This character sits in the same strange and surprising attitude as Rodin's contemplative athlete, with his right elbow on his left thigh — an attitude which makes one think of yoga in connection with his mental exercise. In Rodin's work however this posture plays a significant role: the right arm of this intellectually endowed Hercules is on one wing of the *Gate*, and his left on the other. In view of this function which he fulfils, his role is clearly an important one. In the *Last Judgment* Michelangelo's character is a damned soul lost in a crowd of his fellows. Rodin gave his wretch the position Michelangelo gave to Christ. In other words it is the Christian world (or at least a certain conception of it) which suffers execution, like the *Walking Man*, and if head and heaven are synonymous, the head being the summit of the body, as the heavens are the head of the universe — one could even say that the ruling class is another equivalent of heaven or head. Rodin therefore, by singling out his condemned soul, reverses the social order and announces the liberation of the working classes whose fate hangs no longer on the heavens but on themselves.

Jean-Paul Sartre reproached the impressionists for the optimism of the light colours they were using

STUDY IN MOVEMENT Water-colour Rodin Museum, Paris

ADAM Bronze, 1880 The Art Institute of Chicago, U.S.A.

Eve Marble, 1881 The Art Institute of Chicago, U.S.A.

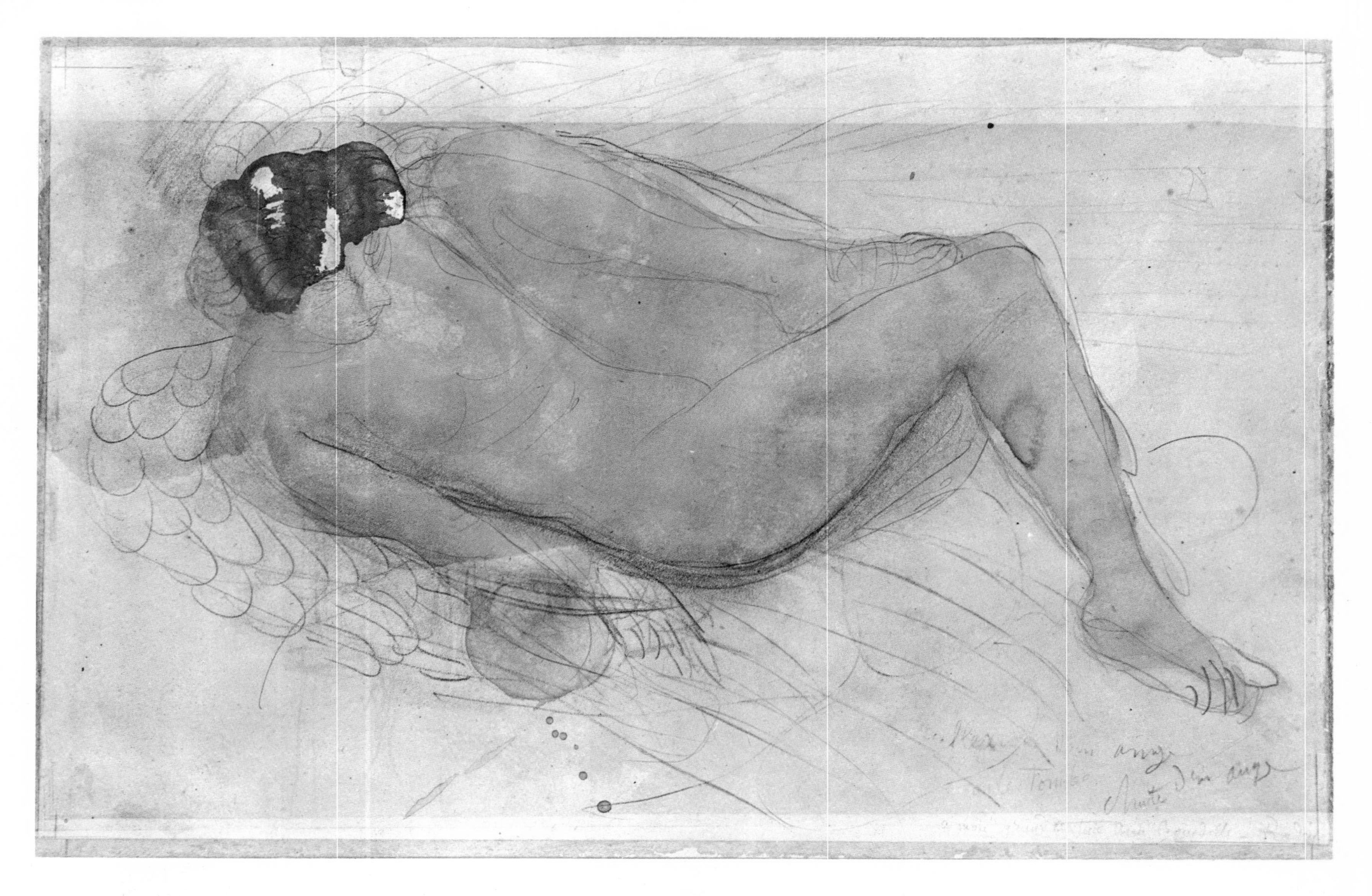

STUDY OF A NUDE Water-colour Bourdelle Museum, Paris

at a moment of tragedy for the working classes. He could not reproach Rodin in the same way, for Rodin is not creating paradise, but a society still in its infernal stage. In any case, inspired as he was by Michelangelo, why did he choose to speak through Dante, instead of in his own name? And if this intermediary was forced on him, why did he accept it with enthusiasm? This enthusiasm has two causes; the choice of hell as his subject was itself significant. Dante wrote his *Paradiso*, but Rodin did not portray it, too. In other words, as with the *Walking Man*, the *Divine Comedy* has been decapitated; from the very beginning, heaven was to be omitted.
" Executioner! " shouted the voice in the rotunda in 1900. Rodin was indeed an executioner, more so than his anonymous accuser perhaps realized. If one compares the scandal of the *Walking Man* in 1900 with that of *Balzac* in 1898, one can see why. In these two works — these two crimes, one might say — Rodin has accomplished a total elimination. Combining the two statues would give one a complete man — a walk ng man with Balzac's head. Rodin had tried this solution with his naked Balzac, and rejected it. The definitive Balzac is, one knows, a head set on a rock, in other words a head without a body. If one adds together the negative elements of the two, the headless giant and the bodiless head, one has a man without either head or body. In other words, man, at least classical man, has been wiped out. Very possibly this was in Rodin's mind when he created the theme of *The Gate of Hell*. In replacing Michelangelo's God with a condemned man, and the prince, or the social class which claimed that its power was God-given, with a workman who draws his strength from the earth, Rodin has destroyed the classical conception of the universe and of society.
But in order to execute grand pieces of sculpture representing an unfortunate in a social and artistic classicism, Rodin had to act with the authority born of a full knowledge of the facts (another reason for his enthusiastic acceptance of Dante's theme). He himself therefore had to be a classic, an illustrator or a descendant of the classics, like Dante or Michelangelo.
How did he become the classical executioner of classicism? The story starts in 1875.

MEDITATION ON MOSES

In that year an energetic-looking Frenchman with knitted brows arrived in Rome from Brussels, where he had been engaged in ornamental sculpture, crossed the threshold of the church of San Pietro in Vinculi and advanced purposefully towards the tomb of Julius II. In the centre of the base of this monument was carved in the marble Michelangelo's Moses. What secrets did Michelangelo transmit to Rodin? Nowadays since one is able to judge their work in its entirety, one can affirm that not only did these two artists unite in depicting *The Thinker* and great cosmosociological scenes such as the *Last Judgment* and *The Gate of Hell*, but that they shared a taste for strength and certain muscular exaggerations. The muscles in the necks of *The Shadows*, and of *The Night* on the tomb of Giulio II de Medici in Florence are the same. Mutilation and decapitation are not inventions of Rodin's, but can also be found in Michelangelo — a sketch for the Medici Madonna is headless, and one arm of the finished statue is so hidden in drapery that from some angles it seems to be missing altogether. If Rodin's unfinished sculptures are famous, Michelangelo's are equally so. The head of *The Day* on the same tomb in Florence is hardly roughed in, while in his marble entitled *Dawn* Rodin reversed this idea, by finishing the head but losing the rest of the body in the stone. Michelangelo's

sensuality is expressed in his love of nakedness (he left all the characters in his *Last Judgment* unclothed, but current modesty made another artist, Daniel de Volterra, cover them with drapery). Rodin did not suffer this misfortune, but he was no less sensual. Men thought he looked like Jove, but women said he had the appeal of a satyr. Some of his statues rank among the most erotic in existence: his famous couple entitled *Le Baiser* (*The Kiss*) on page 32, which is reproduced on the covers of many books on sexual education, is typical. The same sensuality is to be found in *L'Eternel Printemps* (*The Eternal Spring*) on page 49, which dates from 1884, in *L'Eternelle Idole* (*The Eternal Idol*), page 35, 1888, *Fugit Amor* (*Fleeting Love*), page 28, of 1886, *Métamorphoses d'Ovide* (*The Metamorphoses of Ovid*), page 20, of 1886 and *Je suis Belle...* (*I Am Beautiful...*) on page 18, sculpted in 1882, which are just random examples. Ancient sculptors fell in love with their works, and if the story of Pygmalion and Galatea inspired Rodin (page 40), it was because he hardly distinguished between an artistic creation and the physical act. During the last seventeen years of the life of the " Master of Meudon " (so-called after his villa outside Paris) an Austrian doctor was fighting the same battle as he, to rehabilitate sex in an era still choked with modesty and hypocrisy. Sigmund Freud met with the same violent opposition as Rodin. Like Freud, Rodin was introducing a new man, and to do so, to anticipate him — that is, to herald his appearance — he had to mutilate and smash the classical body he so adored. A tragic fate, but Rodin was not the first to suffer thus; Michelangelo had prophesied the same superman — or at least the same metamorphosed humanity — more than three centuries before anyone dared to create his image.
Did the visitor with the knitted brows ponder all this before Michelangelo's Moses in the church of St. Peter-in-chains? Perhaps without realizing its full import he sensed a strange affinity, like that of Delacroix with Rubens, or Cézanne with El Greco. Great innovators need illustrious forerunners both to support them in their daring and to modify their defiance by the mellowing effect of distance. Rodin's celebrated forerunner was always the creator of Moses, as Cézanne's was the Cretan who lived and died at Toledo. Cézanne felt bonds between himself and Rodin. The story is told of a meeting one day between them at Monet's house, when the man who had said of himself "A painter like me only appears once in three centuries " threw himself on his knees before the Olympian-headed sculptor who deserved as much as did Puget the epithet of the French Michelangelo and cried: " You, at least, have triumphed! ". In fact both triumphed equally, though the true success of Cézanne was the posthumous success we know though he did not, of the new schools of painting which are inconceivable without his work, as the true success of Rodin was not his material success (which afforded him his many studios and assistants) but that new school of sculpture which was the offspring of his work. Such success was not shared by El Greco and Michelangelo, neither of whom had anyone to carry on their work. In this sense Cézanne represents El Greco's success, as Rodin is not only the French Michelangelo, but also the Italian's historical justification.
In the church of St. Peter-in-chains in 1875, did the vigorous-looking visitor already realize that he was to give the creator of Julius II's tomb the justification of which history had deprived him, because in the sixteenth century people were not yet ready to look properly at his visual offerings? Undoubtedly Rodin must have had some vague presentiment, but his dominant thought must have been that in order to have the influence and spiritual successors which the famous Florentine lacked he must first become as great a sculptor as he. Why this passionate interest in the Hebrew leader and

Cambodian
Woman
Seated
Water-colour
Rodin Museum
Paris

particularly in his beard? Perhaps because Rodin sensed that he might one day have an equally luxuriant growth, or else because he noticed a gesture of the right hand of the Law-Giver which deflected its flow, so that there is a depression at the level of his stomach which carves out a hollow in his thorax. This concave form he adopted and used, notably in his Eustache de Saint-Pierre. But at that moment he had not yet thought of the group of *Burghers of Calais*, which was the precursor of Etienne-Martin's *Les Demeures*, and only entered his life nine years later. Rather he was remembering the long hours of study of classical works in the Louvre. The ancients did not hollow out their figures, but swelled them. He also remembered the medieval statuary he had studied at Rheims during his journey. Like Michelangelo and unlike the ancient sculptors, the medieval artists made concave figures with corbel-like silhouettes. All at once his face lightened. He had found what he sought. Michelangelo was not what one supposed him to be, the continuer of classical art, but " the last and greatest of the Gothics ", as Rodin was to confide much later to Paul Gsell — a fact which had escaped everyone before him. Thus he who understood the great Florentine so well would perhaps be able to equal him and across the span of the centuries which divided them become his sole spiritual heir and the sole worthy successor of his art.

It was undoubtedly at this moment of exaltation that he conceived the idea of a sculpture whose strange destiny and metamorphoses were to resemble a self-portrait and the symbol of his role in the evolution of western art and thought. This takes us back to Brussels, two years later.

THE AFFAIR OF THE CASTING

The scene took place in January 1877 at the Exhibition of the Cercle Artistique of Brussels, where discussion was centred around a plaster sculpture by a young artist newly returned from Italy, entitled *Le Vaincu* (*The Vanquished*). Primarily this was the figure of a shepherd (Moses had originally been a shepherd). Perhaps this was Rodin's way of approaching Michelangelo's subject, but modifying it — his Moses was young — while remaining within the same realm, for *The Vanquished* is also a memorial of those *Schiavi* (*Slaves*) which the great Florentine regarded as allegories of the cities conquered by Julius II.

How did Rodin's *Vanquished* come to be a peaceful keeper of sheep? By the elimination (a much less serious mutilation than those which were to follow) of the staff which the young peasant held in his right hand to lean on. He is in fact disarmed, like a conquered soldier. This was not however the subject of discussion at the Cercle Artistique. Opinions were divided, some saying that it was a wonderful, vivid piece of sculpture, while others maintained that this was hardly surprising, since it was a cast, meaning that Rodin had contented himself with performing a number of operations which were in no way creative, posing a nude youth and taking a cast of his entire body. On this suspicion burst the scandal of the *Vanquished*, which was to become the scandal of *The Bronze Age* (page 10), when the same statue was exhibited in Paris with the new title a few months later.

Was Rodin guilty? Even if the suspicions of the people in Brussels and Paris in 1877 were well founded, we would not use this term to-day, because ' casting ' has become respectable. Picasso, the young American Segal, the Frenchman Ipousteguy and many others have used this process. Nearer to

WOMAN IN BLUE Water-colour Bourdelle Museum, Paris ▷

à Bourdelle. Rodin

THE WEEPING LION Marble, 1881
Rodin Museum, Paris

THE ETERNAL SPRING Marble, 1885
Metropolitan Museum of Art, New York

M.R
7146

Rodin, between 1910 and 1926 Gaudi introduced castings for the figures of saints and apostles in his decoration of the Sagrada Familia at Barcelona.

So Rodin's accusers were actually making an innovator of him, but he defended himself fiercely against their attacks, because he had other ways of surrendering to nature, through a creative use of improvization and chance.

At the Hôtel Biron in Paris, which became the Rodin Museum, Auguste Rodin used to lie in wait, occasionally making a rapid sketch or one of his famous drawings, recording the gesture of one of the nude models circulating freely in front of him. At this moment no-one had yet heard of improvized music, Max Ernst had not applied his *frottages* and the *tachistes* had not yet started on their spontaneous painting. However in the relationship of artist and model, contrary to the other contemporary sculptors who posed their models in deliberately contrived and lengthily pondered attitudes, Rodin was already using the technique of laissez-faire and improvization.

When the little girl asked him in 1900 why his walking man had no head, he could have replied: " Because the head, which is the seat of reason and will, is no longer enough to grasp beauty ". This leads me to refer to another walking man. Unlike the giant at the World Exhibition, he was normally equipped with a head and two arms. Rodin conceived and executed him at the same time as *The Bronze Age*. Unfortunately, according to some historians, the artistic world has lost track of him. One can easily guess his name. There was a man in the Bible who was to Moses what Rodin wanted to be to Michelangelo — a great successor. In the last three verses of Alfred de Vigny's poem *Moïse* this great successor " pensif et palissant " (" thoughtful and pale ") led the Hebrew people towards the Promised Land which he was to conquer. Joshua. The poet described him as " walking ". How did Rodin express this idea of movement? The answer was to be found in the rotunda in 1900, in full view of the public. It is the metal giant of whom the little girl, the daughter of an art critic, asked why he had no head. Rodin smilingly replied " Because he's walking " and went on to explain " If he had a head, you'd only look at it ".

Rodin well knew the tyranny of the head, and was ready to yield to it. In fact from 1900 on, apart from the modifications made to *The Gate of Hell*, some nude sculptures and a few monuments which revived old themes without much alteration, his main production consisted of a splendid series of portraits reduced to heads and their immediate surroundings. Heads exercise a sway over one's eyes both because they are the seat of the faculty of intelligence on which men pride themselves, and also because they are the best-known part of the body, since they are always open to view. The other parts of the body seem by comparison abstract, or extremely ambiguous. Thus by decapitating his giant Rodin also introduced abstract sculpture.

It is by people's heads that one distinguishes them most surely from each other and heads are therefore not suitable for portraying vague reveries. Nevertheless Rodin has often in his marble sculptures, especially *Puvis de Chavannes*, *Mozart* (page 55) and one of his portraits of Victor Hugo (page 50), tried to take up the challenge and create a head as hazy and evanescent as a slippery chute down which one falls in a dream.

Conversely, by pointing and even exaggerating the characteristics of the other parts of the body, he made them like features, and even spoke of the smile of a trunk or a belly. But the best way to make a trunk or belly smile or grimace, or to make them attractive like faces, is to omit their chief

◁ WOMAN WITH FUR Pencil and Water-colour Rodin Museum, Paris

Nude Woman Seated right Profile
Pencil and Water-colour
Petit Palais
Paris

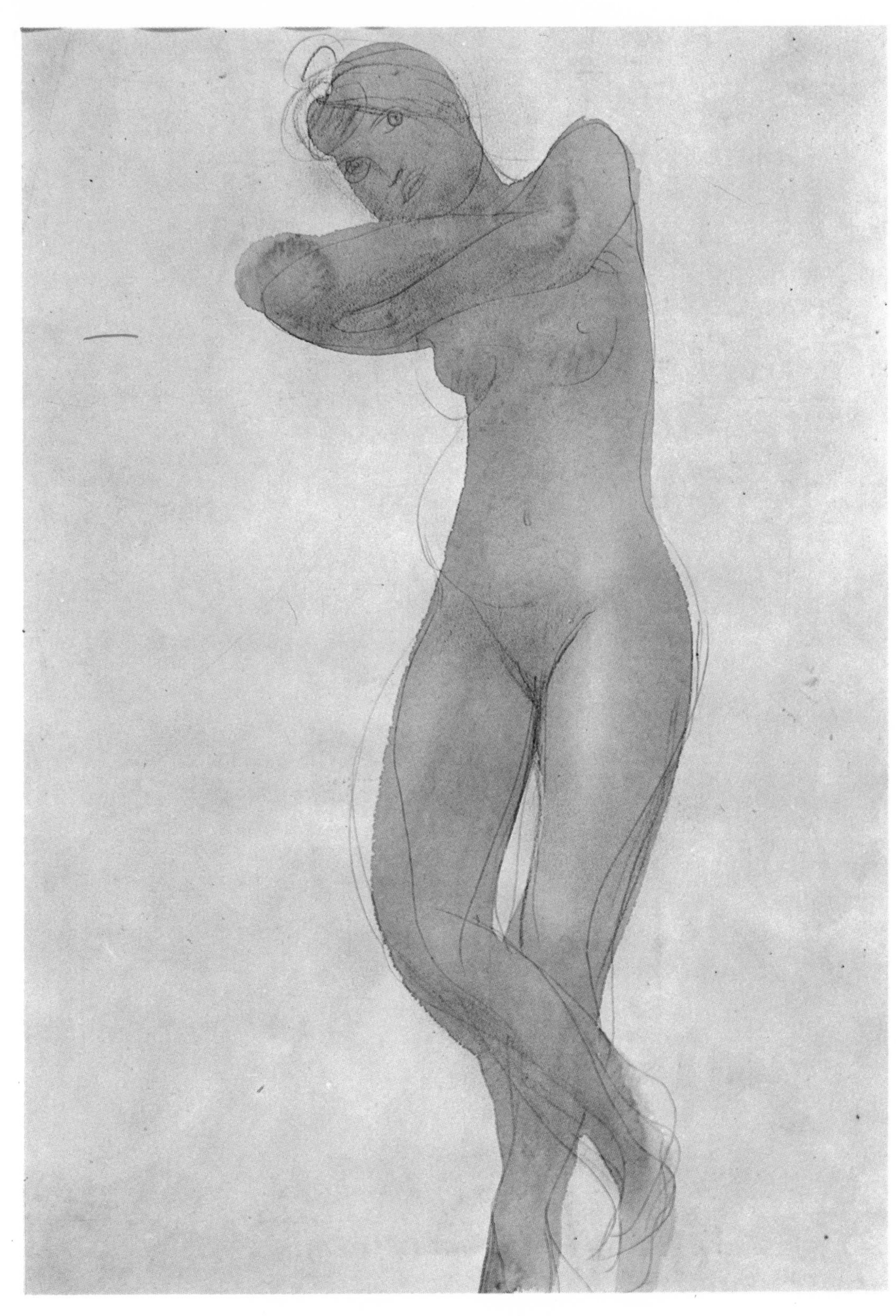

STUDY OF A NUDE Water-colour Bourdelle Museum, Paris

She who was the Beautiful Heaulmière Bronze, 1885 Rodin Museum, Paris rival, the real face. This is why the *Walking Man* has no head and why, among other reasons, Rodin once said " His head is everywhere ", when someone asked him the same question as the little girl. This translation of the head into the body and legs makes a monster as disturbing as the monsters of Picasso and very similar to those created by Miro and Enrico Baj, which consist of a head resting on two hands.

But to the little girl, even though she was the daughter of an art-critic, the bronze giant was headless. Rodin said this was because he was walking; in other words, to make one look at his legs. But his legs are motionless. How do they give this impression of walking which Joshua must give if he is to look like a leader? Rodin did not explain this to the little girl but to an adult who was making a collection of his sayings. As Jean Selz pointed out, the *Walking Man's* left leg is longer than his right. In fact to comply with the rules of anatomy and the movement of walking, the left heel should be raised off the ground, but it is in fact as totally attached to the plinth as the right heel. Rodin explained to Paul Gsell that this was because he had combined many different positions in one — the position with the raised heel and that when the heel touches the ground. Rodin had thus made in this leg what Picasso, Braque and the cubists made in those faces which closely unite frontview and profile. He has simultaneously displayed two views of an object which can in fact only be seen successively, and this was not in 1907, the year when cubism was born, but in 1877, exactly thirty years earlier.

So Rodin is a prophet of cubism, futurism, of the new man who was to rise from the ashes of the old man. He also seems to be more a St. John the Baptist than a Moses or a Joshua. When one considers all that his art foretold, should one not look for his portrait in the face of the Messenger of Christ rather than in that of the conqueror of the Promised Land? In fact these two characters are closely bound together.

THE CONQUEROR OF THE PROMISED LAND

It is worth studying the genealogy of *St. John the Baptist* within Rodin's work. It was carved in 1877, one year after *The Bronze Age*, exhibited at the Salon in 1880 and awarded a Third Prize. It would be the son of the *Walking Man*, who would be a preliminary study for it (but was not shown to the public until twenty years later). Who was the father of the headless man and the grandfather of the Messenger of Christ? Madame Cécile Goldscheider has suggested an answer which shows how Rodin practised the technique of improvization, and may be found in the following anecdote which dates from 1877.

The young sculptor who had caused a scandal when he exhibited *The Vanquished*, that conquered man who was a shepherd and became " Man awakening to nature ", and *The Bronze Age*, was then in Paris, supervising the unpacking of some sculptures which had just arrived from Brussels. He gave a sigh of relief when he saw that *The Bronze Age* was intact, but unfortunately not all the statues were undamaged. Was it a jolt in the train, clumsy handling or bad packing that damaged Joshua so badly? The trunk was broken in two places, at the stomach and at the bottom of the belly, in two horizontal cracks similar to those in *Le Torse d'Homme* (*Male Torso*) at the Petit Palais (page 17) and in the body of the *Walking Man*. The lower limbs were broken at the top of the thighs. These breaks are as clear to see in the sculpture at the Petit Palais as in the walker. To the latter Rodin restored both legs in

Cambodian Dancer
Water-colour
1906
Rodin Museum
Paris

FAUN
AND NYMPH
Water-colour
Rodin Museum
Paris

THE IDYLL OF IXELLES Bronze, 1876 Rodin Museum, Paris

CAMBODIAN
DANCER
Water-colour
1906
lin Museum
Paris

good condition, but to the former only one thigh. The two sculptures are probably cast from the same débris of Joshua, though one of them — the walker — comprises more than the other. Both are headless and armless.

" Executioner " cried the unknown voice.

Rodin might have replied " I'm not the executioner — it's the train, it's the transporter, it's bad luck ". We know he was not averse to collaborating with fortune, but the result is a monster. Rodin in 1877 made a statue of a superbly beautiful young man. How could he accept this monstrous image of a body supported on two legs? The answer is simply that for him all nature — including monsters which like luck and hazard are part of nature — was beautiful. He said repeatedly to Paul Gsell: " In nature everything is beautiful; everything ". Even pain (see cover), even hell (this is one reason for his sculpting *The Gate of Hell*) and even execution and amputation, even pathetic old age as in *She Who Was The Beautiful Heaulmière*. This truth, is such it is, he shows in both its aspects. Beauty is that which looks beautiful (*The Bronze Age*), and also that which looks ugly (the humiliated old woman who in her triumphant youth had been sung by Villon). Rodin extolled everything, old age and youth alike, and found no millionth of an inch in the universe which was not superbly beautiful. This discovery bordered on wisdom, and so at the age of sixty, holding the hand of a little girl who asked him a difficult and even agonizing question, he retained his expression of Olympic serenity, even though he could not repress a muscular contraction in his fingers. Simple intellectual honesty compelled him however to acknowledge that this reconciliation with the universe was a difficult task. Let us assert that ugliness, like evil and wrong, does not exist, as certain philosophers have maintained, yet there is an aspect of ugliness which obsesses us and from which we can hardly tear ourselves away. How can one avoid it? Rodin's answer was in the way in which one looked. " It is not that beauty is missing from before our eyes ", he said to Gsell, " but that our eyes themselves lack beauty ". The best artist is he who best sees this beauty and best transmits his vision to others, that is, he who has the best eyes and the best hands. Hence the importance of hands in Rodin's work. He came to consider a single hand moulded into tiny human bodies — *La Main de Dieu* (*The Hand of God*) on page 53 — as a complete piece of work. His *Burghers of Calais* have huge, strongly expressive hands, which seem to speak. The hand on which *The Thinker* rests his massive head is also enormous. Undoubtedly hands, like faces, are most often visible in everyday life. We know them well, can interpret their movements, or at least most of their movements, and this knowledge and the attention we pay them magnify their size. Hands are also skilled, as is *The Thinker*'s hand; they are the buttress and necessary complement to thought. Thanks to hands the artist, if he is a sculptor, can express his vision and his wisdom.

St. John the Baptist talks with his fingers as much as with his mouth and even with his whole body. He walks like *The Walking Man* and is thus a prophet, for it is enough to walk when all the world stands still to foretell the future. The future he foretells is the future of Joshua, the conquest of the Promised Land; that is, a place where men are not alone, where they wander no longer in the wilderness, where they are reconciled to the world.

Balzac says the same. He is a head poised, to use Miro's phrase, on a mountain. He is a man whose body has become a mountain, a head finally reconciled, for it harmonizes perfectly with the mass of the world.

Caryatide with Stone Marble, 1906 The Art Institute of Chicago, U.S.A.

CAMBODIAN DANCER
Water-colou
1906
Rodin Muse
Paris

How this head became reconciled, *The Walking Man* can teach us: by losing itself. The world has taken its place. This was of course what Rodin was trying to say when he replied " But his head is everywhere ". So *The Walking Man* walks to the rhythm of the universe.

Still the question of how one reaches such great results and such a formidable reconciliation, how such an arduously wrought peace treaty came to the point of being signed, remains unanswered. Rodin replied that this signature is written in the eyes of the world when the world becomes receptive to a certain vision, the vision expressed by his works. What is this potent method of perception?

One day as I looked at *The Thinker* I seemed to realize that the method of perception to which Rodin's work bears witness is that of a colourist. The common denominator to which Rodin reduces everything he sees, to unify it and stamp it with beauty, is a living volume, which in the three-dimensional sphere of sculpture is the equivalent of living colour in the two dimensional sphere of painting. Both have the same enemy: the exigency of clear contour, or ' line ' in current artistic terminology, which is a prerequisite because it is very fragile. The slightest nuance of colour, the slightest vibration of volume upsets it and consequently destroys it, because its definition is clarity. Therefore not all who see vivid volume and colour succeed in grasping contour. Cézanne, who saw colour, said: " Contour escapes me ". Looking at *The Thinker* and seeing its living volume I had exactly the same impression. When I thought I had grasped a line, it escaped me at once, because I could not find its whereabouts nor discover what kind of curve or straight line it was. It wavered, slipped and vanished. Of course one can make beautiful works with clear contours; volume and colour are only the means to obtain this contour which kills them or at best reduces them to a subordinate role. Even if I had not perceived Rodin's colourism when looking at *The Thinker* I would often have been made aware of it. In Rodin's art collection, beside ancient sculptures such as a Roman marble representing Agrippina or the marble copy of Praxiteles's *Satyr*, can be found a painting far ahead of its time which betrays an audacious decision. It is a canvas by a very great colourist, Van Gogh's *Portrait du Père Tanguy* (*Portrait of Father Tanguy*). Rodin had been a painter; his water-colours herald the style of Matisse and Dufy, two other great colourists. Undoubtedly his pictures painted in Belgium are nearer to the style of the *valoriste*, Corot, but at that time colouring sculptures by the manipulation of volumes concerned him more than colouring canvas. Besides he was still seeking himself.

Later, when this search was ended, he was to explain most precisely to Paul Gsell, who devoted a whole chapter of his memoirs to this subject, how sculpture could be coloured without colour by an intense manipulation of the material, so that holes, cuts, scratches, slashes, curlings, crumplings, wounds and scars were not just sadistic manifestations but also the means of giving life and evidence of love of chromatic volume. This love of colour showed itself early in his life, for around 1855 visitors to the Louvre could see in the rooms of the great Venetian colourists a boy of about 15 displaying simultaneously admiration, a wish to shout (at least within himself) " I am a painter, too " and despair. In fact to reproduce these lovely colours of the Venetian school one needs expensive paints, too expensive for the impecunious young man. Some time later, the same visitors saw him again, this time with paper and chalks or charcoal — cheaper materials — copying the old masters. " I got into the habit " Rodin recalled " and that is how I became a sculptor ", but he was still a colourist, that is a man from whom the contours of things escaped.

His vanishing contours, betrayed by their sinuousness and the breaks in their lines, contain the danger

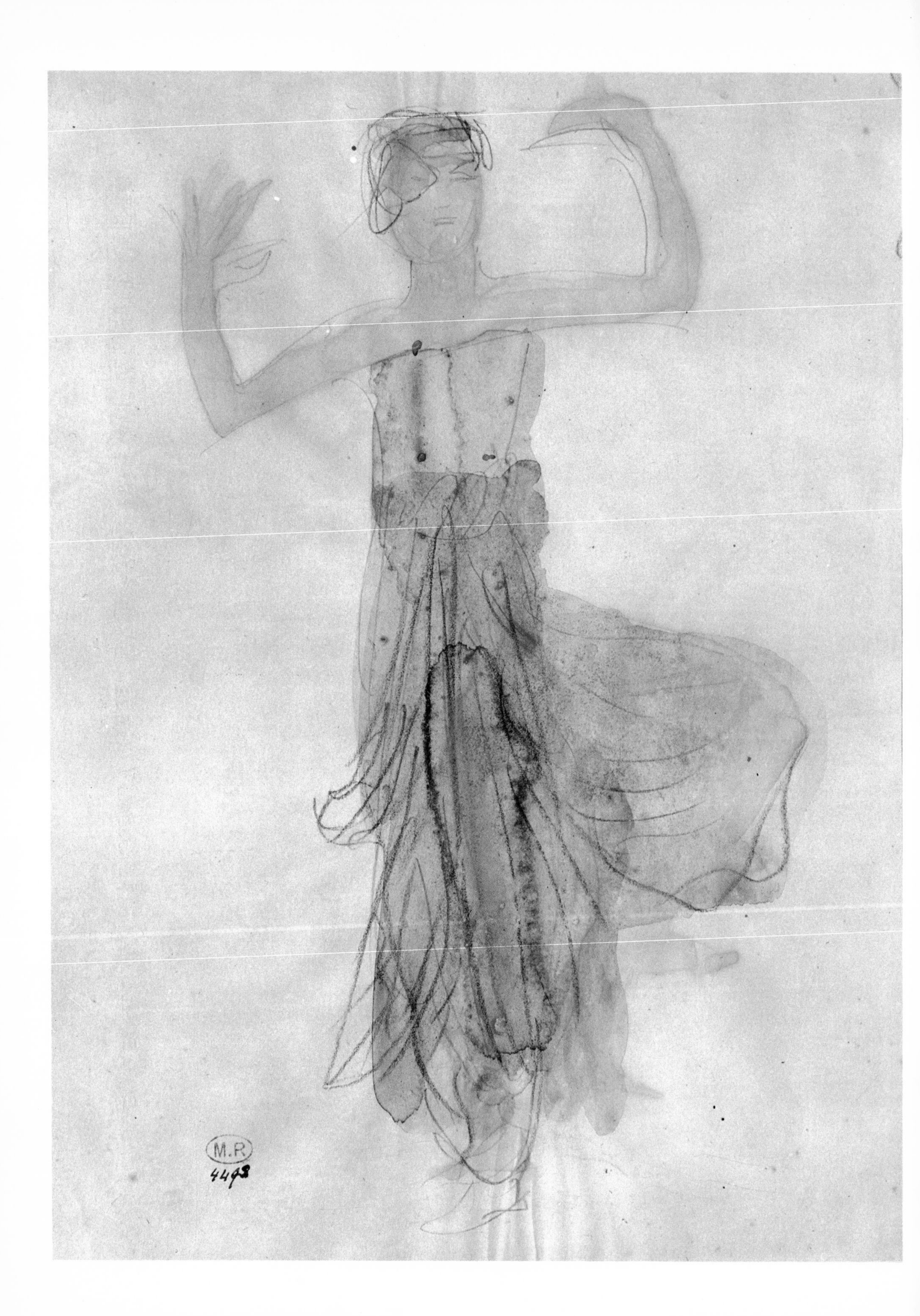

CAMBODIAN DANCER
Water-colour
1906
Rodin Museum
Paris
◁

▷
CAMBODIAN DANCER
Water-colour
1906
Rodin Museum
Paris

of the dissolution of form, and because he avoided this danger Rodin has been compared to the impressionists, who found themselves in the same situation as he, and can be regarded as a forerunner of the informal artists. Rodin walked beneath the threat of dissolution, very near the path trodden by Van Gogh, in whose works forms are retained by a kind of life current which creates huge whirlwinds. In Rodin this function is fulfilled by the gestures of his personages, gestures so striking and emphatic that they seem like letters, like type-characters or simple geometric figures. The square and its diagonal, formed by shoulders and arms, are seen in *Eve* (page 63) and the little *Walking Man* (page 26). A square encloses the *Three Shadows* (page 13) whose arms are three-fold radia. *The Thinker* seen from three-quarter position consists of a zigzag in a semicircle. The arm of *St. John the Baptist* (page 8) form a capital V while the outside extremity of his body and the curve of his left arm form a capital D. *L'Enfant Prodigue* (*The Prodigal Son*) on page 34 is a capital C reversed. There is a false symmetry in the right leg of the man and both legs of the woman in *The Kiss* (page 32) and a rectangular trapezium appears in the arrangement of their arms and bodies (page 33). A small v upside down is to be found in the body which symbolizes *Le Désespoir* (*Despair*), a marble in the City Art Museum of St. Louis (page 22), and the back of the bronze woman in the Rodin Museum who also symbolizes Despair forms a capital C, which is joined to a capital K on its back, made by her arms and legs (page 44). The twisting of the unmutilated *Méditation* (*Meditation*) on page 19 creates a long-handled sickle or a capital M. In *I Am Beautiful* (page 18) there is a capital C reversed and crowned with an N on its side. A capital T askew can be seen in *Le Lion qui pleure* (*The Weeping Lion*) (page 70) and a capital C in his mouth. There is another capital T askew and a reversed Z embracing the bronze version of *The Eternal Spring* (page 49). A small x with two detached curves contains the marble version of the same subject (page 71), in the lower part of which one can see the lines converge. Finally there is the reversed capital Y of the large *Walking Man.* Why has he no head, nor arms? Rodin could reply "Just to make this clear, upside down Y".

THE WALK TO THE STARS

This is the story of a noise, the noise of the rustling of dead leaves heard by men of a far-off age when everyone went naked. It was night and a fire was burning in the forest. The rustling of the leaves drew nearer, when all at once a cry was heard. Into the circle of light burst a headless, armless monster. Another step and he became normal, as the light fell on his face and upper limbs. To the question about his giant's face and arms Rodin could reply "Because I admire Rembrandt, who executes and mutilates, too, by plunging heads or limbs or both into a deep, thick and secret darkness".
From this point of view, that of the chiaroscuro, Rodin's mutilated creations give one's imagination an impression of darkness — volume is light, and everything outside that compact volume is shadow. One receives the same impression and for analogous reasons, from a number of modern works which I describe as "torn". This secretion of shadow, comparable to an octopus's secretion of ink, has the notable advantage of isolating sculpture from its surroundings and protecting it as the octopus protects itself with its inky effusions. It gives sculpture its autonomy in relation to its environs, and especially to architecture.
Rodin must have felt satisfied. He had long been engaged on executing pot-boilers, however accom-

Balzac Bronze, 1893-1897
Rodin Museum, Paris

THE CATHEDRAL
Stone, 1908
Rodin Museum, Paris

plished, and even after the scandal of *The Bronze Age* which made him famous, he accepted a job in the Sèvres factory, where until 1882 he designed vases and cups (page 92) and decorated them himself. His hardest moment was during his stay in Belgium, when he was doing decorative work subject to the requirements of architecture. He must have found it pleasant, a sort of revenge, to liberate the sculptor from the tyranny of the architect.

But this is only one aspect of the secretion of darkness. There is another, even more impressive, because it does not only emanate from mutilation. The pliant forms which result from Rodin's colourism, even in the figures of adults, subtly suggest a soft foetus in the darkness of the womb. The same idea of dark, prenatal life is conjured up both precisely by the *Femme-Poisson* (*The Fish-Woman*) because the foetus within the womb is like a fish in its liquid habitat, and also in a more general sense by the bracket or cave form (which was to be taken up by Pevsner), the cave being another symbol of the womb. Again one sees this similarity to the foetus in his curled-up people, such as *Danaid* (page 23) or the woman in the group entitled *I Am Beautiful* — an obeisance to Baudelaire. This woman is, besides, held up in the air by the hands of an athletic lover (page 18). The foetus is, after all, a passenger.

Those of his sculptures and marbles which were left deliberately unfinished demonstrate equally the theme of gestation, and in this context secrete darkness, in spite of their whiteness, a darkness sometimes deepened by the difficulty of interpretation as in *Ariane* (where are her head and her arm?), but the gestation suggested by these sculptures is either that inverse gestation which puts an end to life and decomposes it into mineral form, thereby confirming the idea of darkness, or else that gestation which is birth. Birth is however a state near to that of uterine darkness, and so the shadows never wholly dissolve.

The same ambiguity, with the same result, is to be found in the amputations when considered from this point of view. They may symbolize castration, which is a kind of death and thus night, but they may also symbolize the cutting of the umbilical cord, that is, the arrival into the world and the achievement of independence, which however is also called birth and though largely a matter of light does not wholly dispel the shadows.

Did the mutilations of *The Walking Man* symbolize castration, the death of an old world, the world of craftsmanship, for instance, whose disappearance Rodin regretted as much as he deplored the rise of industry, saying as he passed a factory from which issued a deafening clatter of machinery "Great forests grow, but make less noise"? Or are these missing parts positive symbols of birth? Rodin's realism was too deep for one to be sure, but his would not have been a wholly optimistic solution. He did however certainly foresee the arrival of a new man, and in spite of his adherence to classicism he guessed that this man was not classical man, for though he pretended to rely on heaven he was in fact only interested in himself. By adding together the missing head of the bronze giant and Balzac's missing body one arrives at the knife without blade or handle which André Breton, to quote Lichtenberg, used to define black humour. Rodin's black humour. What did it consist of, once classical man was gone? In three lovely statements Rilke has given an answer. First he speaks of *The Age of Bronze* which is, it seems to him, enveloped in a closed space, a sort of prenatal space in which the adolescent is still imprisoned as in his mother's womb; then the figure of *St. John the Baptist*, whose gestures

Nɪɢʜᴛ (Pompeian Urn) Sèvres Vase, 1880 Rodin Museum, Paris

widen and dilate the space around him, and thirdly several mutilated statues, including *The Walking Man;* in this case the suggested space is so dilated that it seems to reach the stars.

Rodin should therefore have eliminated heaven and replaced it with another, a new heaven where man would no longer project his image but himself into that space; a heaven on which man no longer depended, but with which he harmonized. So *The Walking Man* whose " head is everywhere " is the walk to the stars, heralding the fantastic pyrotechnics and the discovery of the planets, like so many other " Promised Lands " which we are beginning to witness. Classical man, this man whose sad reign extended well beyond the classical era, the man who withdrew from the world, thus making it a desert and spreading around him endless reproductions of himself, like an opaque screen, is dead, like Nietzsche's God. What remains of him? As Rilke suggested, more remains than has been destroyed. The world remains, an enlarged world, and a new, more lucid man with a deeper or more complex idea of the divine, more able to penetrate the great forces of nature where, said Rodin, provided one has the vision, " all is beautiful ".

LANDSCAPE IN THE FOREST OF SOIGNES Oil-painting, 1872-1876 Rodin Museum, Paris

BIOGRAPHY

1840. On 12th November, François Auguste René Rodin, " the father of modern sculpture ", born in Paris, two days before Claude Monet, " the father of impressionism ", and one year after Cézanne, " the father of modern painting ". His father was a police official who retired in 1861 with the rank of Inspector. Rodin was a bad pupil until he entered the Decorative Arts High School where from 1854 to 1857 he studied drawing from memory under Lecoq de Boisbaudran. He realized his lack of general culture by comparison with his fellow-students and took courses in literature and history at the French College. Showed admiration for Dante. Concurrently with his studies he earned his living with decorative art, castings, and designs for cabinet-work and jewelry.

1860. His first portrait, of his father, Jean-Baptiste.

1862. Death of his sister Maria, aged 22. Despair. Entered a religious order. A year later executed portrait of the Superior, R. P. A. Eymard, who sent him home, saying that he had more talent for sculpture than for the religious life.

1864. An old porter he met in the street served as model for his *Man with Broken Nose*, his first truly original work. Formed a liaison with a seamstress, Marie-Rose Beuret, who bore him a son in 1866 and remained his life-long companion. Though his first sketches had been corrected by Carpeaux and he had taken lessons from Barye, he now entered the service of a mediocre sculptor, Carrier-Belleuse, for whom he worked until 1870.

1870. Enlisted in the National Guard. Discharged on account of short-sightedness.

1871. Carrier-Belleuse asked him to assist with the decoration of the Commercial Exchange in Brussels.

1872. Temporary estrangement from Carrier-Belleuse. Remained in Brussels, though penniless and hungry.

1873. 12th February. Entered into a contract with Van Rasbourg, whereby this competent but unimaginative sculptor was to take the credit for Rodin's works executed in Belgium.

1875. Winter. Travelled to Italy, via Rheims, Pontarlier, Lausanne, Geneva and Mont-Cenis. In Italy travelled through Turin, Genoa (where he saw the works of Puget, " the French Michelangelo "), Pisa and Florence to Rome, where he discovered Michelangelo, of whom he said: " It is he who has freed me from academic sculpture ".

1876. Returned to Belgium, and probably sculpted *Joshua*. Created *The Vanquished*, the name of which he later changed to *The Bronze Age*.

1877. The scandal of *The Vanquished*, in Brussels. Return to Paris, where occurred the scandal of *The Bronze Age*. Date of creation of *The Walking Man*.

1878. *Head of Man with Broken Nose* rediscovered by Jules Dubois, who revealed its exceptional quality. Rodin commissioned by the sculptor Laouste to execute the great decorative scrolls on the Trocadero Palace for the World Exhibition.

1879. Carrier-Belleuse, become Director of the Sèvres factory, engaged him to design vases and cups (until 1882).

1880. Presentation of *St. John the Baptist Preaching* at the Salon. Purchase of the bronze of *The Bronze Age* by the State. On 16th August, Rodin received commission for *The Gate of Hell*. Occupied two studios at the Marble Warehouse. Year of *The Thinker, Adam or the First Man* and *The Three Shadows*.

1881. *Eve, Ugolin, The Weeping Lion, The Fallen Caryatide carrying her stone.*

1882. *La Douleur* (*Pain*), *La Femme accroupie* (*Crouching Woman*).

1882-3. Became acquainted with Léon Claudel's family. Met Gambetta, many political men and Victor Hugo, of whom he sculpted a bust. Beginning of his passion for Camille Claudel, sister of Paul and herself a sculptress.

1884-6. *The Burghers of Calais.*

1885. *Dawn*

1886. *The Kiss; Thought.*

1888. Illustration of *Les Fleurs du Mal* for the publisher Gallimard. *The Walking Man* cast in bronze.

1889. Monument to Claude Lorrain. Commissioned to execute monument to Victor Hugo. Meeting with Medaro Rosso, followed by a quarrel, since both claimed to have been the first to use impressionism in sculpture.

1890. Rodin invited by the Commission for Works of Art to revise his draft for the monument to Victor Hugo.

1891. Commissioned to execute the monument to Balzac. Rodin was then 51 — the age at which the novelist died.

1893. Rodin due to complete his *Balzac*, which was by then in its naked, paunchy form. He refused to regard it as finished, and the " Balzac affair " began.

1895. 3rd June. Erection and unveiling of the *Burghers of Calais* in their native town.

1897. Purchase of " La Villa des Brillants " (" The House of Diamonds ") at Meudon. Final version of *Balzac* (the Balzac-mountain). End of his liaison with Camille Claudel.

1898. *Balzac* scandal, when it was rejected by the Society of Men of Letters. Beginning of his monument to President Sarmiento, at Buenos Aires.

1900. During the World Exhibition, Rodin showed two hundred works in a rotunda-shaped pavillon, among them *The Walking Man*, exhibited for the first time since its creation in 1877.

1902. The caster Eugène Rudier summoned to Rodin's studio every morning at eight. On 2nd September, Rilke rang his doorbell at No. 182, Rue de l'Université.

1904. Rodin refunded the money given by the State for *The Gate of Hell*, the copyright of which he retained. Decoration of entrance-hall of the villa " La Sapinière " at Evian.

1905. Rilke became his secretary in the middle of September. Charles Morice and Mario Meunier, one of the best translators of Plato, had been his predecessors. Of Rodin's assistant sculptors, three were to become famous — Pompon, Bourdelle and Despiau.

1907. Took up residence at the Hôtel Biron.

1908. Monument to Henri Becque.

1911. Gustave Cogniot and Judith Cladel conceived the idea of making the Hôtel Biron into the Rodin Museum. This was finally realized in the laws of 22nd December, 1917 and 23nd June, 1918.

1915. Second journey to Italy.

1917. 14th February. Death of Rose Beuret, whom he had married some time previously. Having been born in November, Rodin also died in November (17th), of lung congestion, at the age of 77.

BIBLIOGRAPHY

GEFFROY, Gustave. *Auguste Rodin*. His artistic life. E. Dentu, Paris, 1893.

MORICE, Charles. *Rodin*. Octavo. H. Floury, Paris, 1900.

COQUIOT, Gustave. *Le vrai Rodin* (*The True Rodin*). Octavo. Paris, 1913.

RILKE, Rainer-Maria. *Auguste Rodin*. Leipzig, 1913.

BOURDELLE, Antoine. *L'Art et Rodin* (*Art and Rodin*). Geneva, 1919.

HAVELAAR, J. *Auguste Rodin*. 160. Leiden, 1920.

GRAPPE, Georges. *Catalogue du Musée Rodin* (*Catalogue of the Rodin Museum*). Paris, 1927.

RIOTOR, Léon. *Rodin*. Alcan, Paris, 1927.

RILKE, Rainer-Maria. *Lettres à Rodin* (*Letters to Rodin*). Paris, 1928.

GRAPPE, Georges. *Le Musée Rodin* (*The Rodin Museum*). Octavo. Paris, 1934.

CLADEL, Judith. *Rodin, sa vie glorieuse et inconnue* (*Rodin, his glorious and unknown life*). Grasset, Paris, 1936.

BOEHMER, Günter. *Rodin*. Octavo. Weise, Berlin, 1938.

MARTINIE, Henri. *Rodin*. Braun, Paris, 1952.

GOLDSCHEIDER, Cécile. *Rodin, sa vie, son œuvre, son héritage* (*Rodin, his life, his work, his heritage*). Paris Productions, Paris, 1962-63.

Catalogue of Rodin Sculpture Exhibition. Museum of Modern Art, New York, 1962.

BORNIBUS, Jacques. *Auguste Rodin*. Gallerie Claude Bernard, Paris, 1963.

SELZ, Jean. *Rodin*, in " Découverte de la Sculpture Moderne" (" Discovery of Modern Sculpture "). Guide du Livre, Lausanne, 1963.

WRITINGS BY RODIN

RODIN, Auguste. *L'Art* (*Art*), conversations recorded by Paul Gsell. Grasset, Paris, 1911; Mermod, Lausanne, 1946; Grasset, Paris, 1951.

RODIN, Auguste. *Les Cathédrales de France* (*The Cathedrals of France*). Quarto. Armand Colin, Paris, 1941.

ILLUSTRATIONS